BUDDHISM
PLAIN AND SIMPLE

Steve Hagen

BUDDHISM
PLAIN AND SIMPLE

The Practice of Being Aware,
Right Now, Every Day

TUTTLE Publishing

Tokyo | Rutland, Vermont | Singapore

Published by Tuttle Publishing, an imprint of Periplus Editions (HK) Ltd.

www.tuttlepublishing.com

The illustration on page 30 is reprinted from John McCrone's book *The Ape That Spoke,* published in the United Kingdom in 1990 by Macmillan General Books, and copyright 1990 by John McCrone. The American edition was published in 1991 by William Morrow and is copyright 1991 by John McCrone.

Library of Congress Catalog Card number: 97061735.

ISBN: 978-0-8048-4336-2

Distributed by

North America, Latin America & Europe
Tuttle Publishing
364 Innovation Drive, North Clarendon, VT 05759-9436 U.S.A.
tel: 1 (802) 773-8930; fax: 1 (802) 773-6993
info@tuttlepublishing.com; www.tuttlepublishing.com

Asia Pacific
Berkeley Books Pte Ltd
61 Tai Seng Avenue #02-12, Singapore 534167
tel: (65) 6280-1330; fax: (65) 6280-6290
inquiries@periplus.com.sg; www.periplus.com

Japan
Tuttle Publishing
Yaekari Building, 3F, 5-4-12 Osaki, Shinagawa-ku, Tokyo 141-0032
tel: (81) 3 5437-0171; fax: (81) 3 5437-0755
sales@tuttle.co.jp; www.tuttle.co.jp

16 15 14 13   10 9 8 7 6 5 4 3 2 1   1306RP
Printed in China

TUTTLE PUBLISHING® is a registered trademark of Tuttle Publishing, a division of Periplus Editions (HK) Ltd.

With gratitude I dedicate this book to all beings.

Acknowledgments

Thanks to all my teachers.

This book resulted from classes
I taught over the past few years.
My thanks to all my students. Without them
this book would not have come to be.

And a special thanks to Scott Edelstein, my
longtime friend and literary advisor, who helped
me put this book together.

Contents

Foreword to This New Edition

When my teacher, Dainin Katagiri, died in 1990, I was at work on my first book, *Why the World Doesn't Seem to Make Sense*. I had no plans at that time to take on students, let alone start a Zen center. But after Katagiri Roshi's death, people began showing up at my door. Before long I was holding study groups and, soon after, teaching courses out of my home. One thing led to another, and within a few years, Dharma Field, the meditation center in Minneapolis where I now teach, was born.

For basic courses, we used *What the Buddha Taught* by Walpola Rahula as a text. It's a wonderful little book that I still regard as an excellent supplement to *Buddhism Plain and Simple*. But it wasn't exactly what people most needed.

I wanted to find a book that presented *simply* and in *plain* English what the Buddha taught. Since nothing like that was available at the time, I wrote such a book myself—the one you're holding now.

While *Buddhism Plain and Simple* has been generally well received, there is one recurring criticism of it that is based on a misunderstanding. I'd like to clear that up here.

Because the word "simple" is in the title, some people have taken it to mean "elementary," or "easy"—i.e., that this book presents a simplified, dumbed-down look at Buddhism. That's not what this book is at all.

What the Buddha taught is utterly profound, and *Buddhism Plain and Simple* in no way dilutes it. On the contrary, this book presents his message plainly and simply, in its full strength and subtlety. It offers readers just what the Buddha pointed out, without the complications of teachings that came along later.

The word "plain" in the title also refers to the fact that this book is in plain English—the English that you and I speak every day. No foreign or arcane terms are used, except in a couple of instances where there's no counterpart in English.

Even then, I've avoided non-English words whenever possible. For example, the word *karma* does not appear in this book, even though there is much discussion of *karma* in its pages. Instead, I've used phrases such as "willed action" and "leaning mind." These get at the subtle point the Buddha was making, while avoiding the inaccuracies that the word "karma" has recently taken on here in the West.

Buddhism Plain and Simple was first published in 1997. Since then I changed the first sentence of the introduction to reflect the passage of time. Otherwise, though, the text of this edition is unchanged from that of the original volume.

May this book help cultivate a deep appreciation for what the Buddha left us.

Steve Hagen
January, 2013

Introduction

As the new millennium dawns, most of us have lost faith in our ancient storybook versions of the world. With the development of science, many of us have come to see the universe as an inconceivably strange, vast, complex, impersonal, multi-dimensional, and perhaps meaningless realm of mind and matter.

We may feel forced to deal with this loss of faith by going to one of two wretched extremes. Either we blind ourselves to our predicament and attempt to escape via drugs or alcohol or our careers or any of innumerable belief systems, or we face the woeful prospect that we're intelligent creatures living in a meaningless world.

Many of us act as though we could find fulfillment if only we possessed enough money, enough security, enough respect, enough love, enough faith, enough education, enough power, enough peace, enough knowledge, enough . . . something.

There are others among us, however, who don't (or can't) buy into this. They sense that real security is impossible to attain. For they know that even if we could manage to accumulate all we desire, it will be inevitably taken from us by death. Our mortality looms above us, as terrifying as it is certain. We seem utterly stumped. How can we possibly find peace under these conditions?

Not only do we feel imprisoned by our ignorance, we seem doomed to remain that way. As Yang Chu, the fourth century B.C.E. Chinese philosopher put it:

> We move through the world in a narrow groove, preoccupied with the petty things we see and hear, brooding over our prejudices, passing by the joys of life without even knowing that we have missed anything. Never for a moment do we taste the heady wine of freedom. We are as truly imprisoned as if we lay at the bottom of a dungeon, heaped with chains.

What is the basic human problem that no apparent remedy will cure? What is our existence all about? How can we ever possibly comprehend the whole of it? And yet isn't knowledge of the Whole—knowledge that's not relative, or dependent on changing conditions—precisely what would be required to free us from the doubts and dilemmas that cause us so much pain and anxiety?

We long to be free from our confusion and discontent, not to have to live out our lives chained helplessly to uncertainty and fear. Yet we often do not realize that it's precisely our confused state of mind that binds us.

There is a way to move beyond this ignorance, pessimism, and confusion, and to experience—rather than comprehend—Reality as a Whole. This experience is not based on any conception or belief; it is direct perception itself. It's *seeing* before signs appear, before ideas sprout, before falling into thought.

It's called enlightenment. It's nothing more or less than *seeing* things as they are rather than as we wish or believe them to be.

This liberation of mind—this direct awareness of Reality as a Whole—is fully accessible to anyone willing to attend to their actual experience.

Twenty-five hundred years ago in India a man named Gautama experienced this liberation. He devoted the remainder of his life to teaching others how to experience the same freedom of mind. After he awakened from the crippling ignorance that kept him from knowing what was actually going on, he became known as the Buddha—the "awakened one."

When the Buddha was asked to sum up his teaching in a single word, he said, "awareness." This is a book about awareness. Not awareness of something in particular, but awareness itself—being awake, alert, in touch with what is actually happening. It's about examining and exploring the most basic questions of life. It's about relying on the immediate experience of this present moment. It's not about belief, doctrine, formula, or tradition. It's about freedom of mind.

The Buddha learned to see directly into the nature of experience. As a result of his teaching and his life, a new religion arose and spread throughout the world. In the process, like all religions, Buddhism accumulated (and generated) a variety of beliefs, rituals, ceremonies, and practices. As it spread from country to country, it acquired a wide variety of cultural trappings: special clothes and hats, statues, incense, gongs, bells, whistles—even peculiar architectural forms, icons, and symbols. This book leaves all that behind.

Rituals, ceremonies, prayers, and special outfits are inevitable, but they do not—they cannot—express the heart of what the

Buddha taught. In fact, all too often, such things get in the way. They veil the simple wisdom of the Buddha's words, and distract us from it.

This is a major problem, and not just for those of us raised in the West. It is not easy to know where Buddhism ends and Asian culture begins, or to distinguish the original and authentic teachings of the Buddha from what was added later by people with less acute insight. As a result, many Americans and Europeans genuinely believe that Buddhism is about worshipping Buddha, or bowing and wearing robes, or working oneself into a trance, or coming up with answers to bewildering riddles, or past and future incarnations.

Buddhism is not about these beliefs and practices. The observations and insights of the Buddha are plain, practical, and eminently down-to-earth. They deal exclusively with *here* and *now*, not with theory, speculation, or belief in some far-off time or place. Because these teachings remain focused on this moment— even as you read this—they remain relevant, and of profound value, to every culture and every person who investigates them seriously. It is to these uncluttered, original insights and observations that this book returns.

This book is divided into three parts. In Part One, we'll focus on the primary teachings of the Buddha, which he called the four truths of existence. In Part Two, we'll focus in greater detail on the fourth of these truths. Here the Buddha lays out a path—a practical and effective way of life—by which we can understand and deal with the world as we find it. And in Part Three, we'll look more closely still to magnify the first two aspects of this path. These two aspects comprise the wisdom teachings of the Buddha, those that deal with human intent and awareness.

For people investigating Buddhism for the first time, *Buddhism Plain and Simple* offers a clear, straightforward look at the wisdom and guidance of an enlightened teacher who lived some 2500 years ago but whose teachings remain as vital and penetrating today as ever. For people already familiar with Buddhism, including long-time practitioners, this book provides a long-needed over-view of Buddhism's essentials, free of the fetters and cultural trap-pings that have accumulated over twenty-five centuries. For every person with a desire to see deeply into the nature of existence, it is a call to awakening.

The Journey Into Now

The man known to us as Buddha lived in northern India (present-day Nepal) in the sixth century B.C.E. Originally named Gautama, he was the only son of a wealthy king who ruled a small country. As a boy and adolescent, Gautama lived a pampered and sheltered life in his father's palace. His father made sure that Gautama received the best of everything: the finest clothes, the best education, and plenty of servants to do his bidding.

Gautama's life was so sheltered, in fact, that he knew nothing of sickness, death, or human suffering until, as a young adult, he heard about death from a servant. Suddenly, for the first time, he was confronted with the reality that human life inevitably entails illness, old age, and death. He was unable to deny or put aside this newfound knowledge, which soon began to trouble him more and more. What was the point of human life, he asked himself, if it was so transient, so uncertain, and so filled with suffering?

The question haunted him until he could no longer enjoy the passing pleasures of his life of luxury. He decided to leave his family's home and relinquish his chance to become king, for he had come to see power and wealth as a veneer over a life that had sorrow and loss at its foundation. He chose instead to devote his time and energy to finding a way to extricate himself from the universal despair that seemed to form the very ground of human existence.

For six years he wandered the valley of the Ganges River, learning the various systems and practices of the great religious teachers of his day. Though he was a good student who quickly mastered whatever he was taught, he found nothing in these teachings and practices that satisfied him, nothing that dispelled the deep sorrow that filled his heart and mind. So he left the teachers and went his own way.

And then, while seated under a tree, Gautama experienced enlightenment. At last he thoroughly understood the human problem, its origin, its ramifications, and its solution.

From then on he was known as the Buddha, which means "the awakened one." For the next forty-five years he taught the way of enlightenment to men and women, nobles and peasants, the learned and the illiterate, the moral and the base, without making the slightest distinction among them. His teaching of liberation from human suffering and despair is universal, and to this day it remains open to anyone who examines it, understands it, and puts it to the test.

One day, soon after the Buddha's enlightenment, a man saw the Buddha walking toward him. The man had not heard of the Buddha, but he could see that there was something different about the man who was approaching, so he was moved to ask, "Are you a god?"

The Buddha answered, "No."

"You're a magician, then? A sorcerer? A wizard?"

"No."

"Are you some kind of celestial being? An angel, perhaps?"

Again the Buddha said, "No."

"Well, then, what are you?"

The Buddha replied, "I am awake."

The Buddha never considered himself to be something other than a human being—only someone who was fully awake. He never claimed to be a god, or to be inspired by God, or to have access to any occult or supernatural power. He attributed his realization and understanding solely to human endeavor and human ability.

We call Gautama "the Buddha," but many other buddhas, many other awakened human beings, exist, and have existed. And every buddha—past, present, and future—is a human being, not a god.

Buddha is not someone you pray to, or try to get something from. Nor is a buddha someone you bow down to. A buddha is simply a person who is awake—nothing more or less.

Buddhism is not a belief system. It's not about accepting certain tenets or believing a set of claims or principles. In fact, it's quite the opposite. It's about examining the world clearly and carefully, about testing everything and every idea. Buddhism is about *see-*

ing. It's about knowing rather than believing or hoping or wishing. It's also about not being afraid to examine anything and everything, including our own personal agendas.

Not least of all, of course, we must examine the Buddha's teaching itself. The Buddha himself invited people on all occasions to test him. "Don't believe me because you see me as your teacher," he said. "Don't believe me because others do. And don't believe anything because you've read it in a book, either. Don't put your faith in reports, or tradition, or hearsay, or the authority of religious leaders or texts. Don't rely on mere logic, or inference, or appearances, or speculation."

The Buddha repeatedly emphasized the impossibility of ever arriving at Truth by giving up your own authority and following the lights of others. Such a path will lead only to an opinion, whether your own or someone else's.

The Buddha encouraged people to "know for yourselves that certain things are unwholesome and wrong. And when you do, then give them up. And when you know for yourselves that certain things are wholesome and good, then accept them and follow them."

The message is always to examine and *see* for yourself. When you *see* for yourself what is true—and that's really the only way that you can genuinely know anything—then embrace it. Until then, just suspend judgment and criticism.

The point of Buddhism is to *just see.* That's all.

We cannot approach Buddhism, or begin any real inquiry into Truth, with any assumption or belief whatsoever. We must be willing to see things as they are, rather than as we hope, wish, or expect them to be.

Authentic Buddhism, therefore, begins with fact. It starts with perception—direct experience.

Real Buddhism is not really an "ism." It's a process, an awareness, an openness, a spirit of inquiry—not a belief system, or even (as we normally understand it) a religion. It is more accurate to call it "the teaching of the awakened," or the *buddha-dharma*. Since the focus of this book is on the teaching of the awakened and not on any sectarian presentation, from here on I will usually use the term "buddha-dharma" rather than "Buddhism."

The teaching of the Buddha does not take what is set down in writing too seriously. Buddhist writings (including this book) can be likened to a raft. A raft is a very handy thing to carry you across the water, from one shore to another. But once you've reached the other shore, you no longer need the raft. Indeed, if you wish to continue your journey beyond the shore, you must leave the raft behind.

Our problem is that we tend to fall in love with the raft. Before long we think, "This has been a very good raft; it has served me well. I want to hang on to it and take it with me as I continue my journey." But if we hang on to Buddhist teachings—or any teachings—they will ultimately become a hindrance. Buddhist teachings and writings can assist you, but you won't find Truth in them, as if Truth somehow resided in the Buddha's words. No words—Buddha's, mine, or anyone else's—can *see* for you. You must do that for yourself, as Buddha did while seated under a tree a hundred generations ago.

Buddha's words can also be likened to a finger pointing at the moon. His teachings can point to Truth, but they cannot *be* Truth. Buddhas—people who are awake—can only point the way.

We cannot hold Truth with words. We can only *see* it, experience it, for ourselves.

If you point out the moon to a cat, she probably won't look at the sky; she'll come up and sniff your finger. In a similar fashion, it's easy for us to become fascinated by a particular teaching, or teacher, or book, or system, or culture, or ritual. But the buddha-dharma—the teaching of the awakened—directs us to focus not on the pointing finger, but on the experience of Truth itself.

Buddhism is sometimes called a non-historical religion. In other words, it doesn't tell a story of creation, or speculate that we're heading toward a heaven or afterlife of some kind. Indeed, the buddha-dharma does not speak of beginnings or ends at all. It's more a religion of middles; in fact, it is often called the middle way.

The buddha-dharma would have you start with what is given in your direct experience. It will not ask you to accept a belief, or to attempt to account for some presumed or imagined thing. The buddha-dharma does not ask you to accept particular explanations of how things are. Truth does not need any explanation. It only needs to be *seen*.

The Buddha said that the human condition is like that of a person shot with an arrow. It is both painful and urgent. But instead of getting immediate help for our affliction, we ask for details about the bow from which the arrow was shot. We ask who made the arrow. We want to know about the appearance and background of the person who strung the bow. We ask about many things—inconsequential things—while overlooking our immediate problem. We ask about origins and ends, but we leave this moment forgotten. We leave it forgotten even though we live in it.

We must first learn how to journey into now.

Part One

THE PERENNIAL PROBLEM

1

The Human Situation

I magine that you see people seated at a sumptuous banquet. Long tables piled high with delicacies are spread out before them. A dazzling and mouth-watering array of foods, perfectly prepared, is steaming and glistening and sizzling right in front of their eyes, easily within reach.

But the people seated at this feast aren't eating. In fact, their plates are empty. They haven't helped themselves to so much as a crumb. They've been seated at this banquet for a long time now. And they're slowly and steadily starving to death.

They're starving not because they can't partake of the wonderful feast, or because eating is forbidden, or difficult, or harmful. They're starving because they don't realize that food is what they need. They don't recognize the sharp, urgent pains in their stomachs as hunger. They don't see that what they need to do, all they need to do, is enjoy the feast that's right in front of them.

This is our basic human situation. Most of us sense that some- thing is amiss with our lives. But we haven't any idea what our problem really is, or what we should do about it. We may see— perhaps dimly—that the food is there before us, but we don't con- nect it to the pain inside us, even as that pain grows sharper and more fierce.

We long for something. We feel pain and loss. We suffer. Every- thing we need to alleviate this dissatisfaction is right here before us. Yet we don't realize it.

According to the buddha-dharma, this sad state of affairs, this profound and ongoing dissatisfaction, is the first truth of existence. All the pain we bring to ourselves and others—the hatred, the war- ring, the groveling, the manipulation—is our own doing. It comes out of our own hearts and minds, out of our own confusion.

Furthermore, if we don't *see* exactly what the problem is, we're going to perpetuate it. We're going to teach our children our con- fusion, and we'll go on, generation after generation, doing more of the same to ourselves and to each other.

When the Buddha looked honestly into his own heart and mind, he realized this, just as countless others have realized it since. Each of these people saw for themselves that their suffering, and the means to stop it, lay within themselves.

This is not to say that we should expect to be free of problems, or that if only we behave properly things will go as we would like. No person's life—including Buddha's—ever is, was, or will be free of difficulty. The buddha-dharma does not promise to make our lives problem-free. Rather, it urges us to examine the nature of our problems, what they are and where they come from. The buddha- dharma is not an armchair philosophy. It isn't pipe dreaming. It's about getting down to basics and acting on them.

There is an old story about a man who came to see the Buddha because he had heard that the Buddha was a great teacher. Like all of us, he had some problems in his life, and he thought the Buddha might be able to help him straighten them out.

He told the Buddha that he was a farmer. "I like farming," he said, "but sometimes it doesn't rain enough, and my crops fail. Last year we nearly starved. And sometimes it rains too much, so my yields aren't what I'd like them to be."

The Buddha patiently listened to the man.

"I'm married, too," said the man. "She's a good wife . . . I love her, in fact. But sometimes she nags me too much. And sometimes I get tired of her."

The Buddha listened quietly.

"I have kids," said the man. "Good kids, too . . . but sometimes they don't show me enough respect. And sometimes . . ."

The man went on like this, laying out all his difficulties and worries. Finally he wound down and waited for the Buddha to say the words that would put everything right for him.

Instead the Buddha said, "I can't help you."

"What do you mean?" said the astonished man.

"Everybody's got problems," said the Buddha. "In fact, we've all got eighty-three problems, each one of us. Eighty-three problems, and there's nothing you can do about it. If you work really hard on one of them, maybe you can fix it—but if you do, another one will pop right into its place. For example, you're going to lose your loved ones eventually. And you're going to die some day. Now there's a problem, and there's nothing you, or I, or anyone else can do about it."

The man became furious. "I thought you were a great teacher!" he shouted. "I thought you could help me! What good is your teaching, then?"

The Buddha said, "Well, maybe it will help you with the eighty-fourth problem."

"The eighty-*fourth* problem?" said the man. "What's the eighty-fourth problem?"

Said the Buddha, "You want to not have any problems."

We think we have to deal with our problems in a way that exterminates them, that distorts or denies their reality. But in doing so, we try to make Reality into something other than what it is. We try to rearrange and manipulate the world so that dogs will never bite, accidents will never happen, and the people we care about will never die. Even on the surface, the futility of such efforts should be obvious.

While I was working on this book, a good friend of mine died—suddenly, inexplicably, with no warning. He was laughing with friends only moments before. He simply walked across the lawn to his front steps, sat down, and died.

Rick was kind, generous, and well-loved by many. He had a happy, solid marriage and left behind a loving wife and three small children. He was 36 years old and, so far as he and anyone else knew, he was in excellent health.

For me, and for others who knew him, his death was very sad. Very shocking. Very unexpected. And very swift. I miss him greatly, and have shed tears with his family and the many friends who loved him.

This is human life. We cannot lose sight of it. Weeds will flourish, though we hate them and wish them gone; flowers will fall, though we love them and long for them to remain.

Human life is characterized by dissatisfaction. It's right here with us. This is the buddha-dharma's first truth of human life. How do we deal with this reality? Should we pretend—or hope—that what we love is not going to die? The awakened would answer with a decisive "no."

The buddha-dharma is grounded in Reality. It is not pie in the sky, or wishful thinking, or a denial of what human life is. There's no attempt to cover up, to gloss over, to reinterpret the facts.

It's imperative to recognize that our dissatisfaction originates within us. It arises out of our own ignorance, out of our blindness to what our situation actually is, out of our wanting Reality to be something other than what it is. Our longing, our craving, our thirsting for something other than Reality is what dissatisfies us.

The second truth of the buddha-dharma, then, is that this dissatisfaction arises within us.

The third truth is that we can realize the origin of our dissatisfaction, and can thus put an end to its most profound and existential forms.

The fourth truth, which I will take up shortly, offers us a means to experience just such a realization. This realization is sometimes called *nirvana* or enlightenment. A more accurate description, however, might simply be freedom of mind.

We often cast our spiritual quest —our grappling with fundamental human issues—as a journey. But the kind of journey we'll embark upon now is not a journey in the usual sense of the word.

Generally we think of a journey as involving movement and direction, either going out somewhere into the world or else leading inward, into the self. But in Buddhism our journey must go nowhere—neither in nor out. Rather, ours is a journey into nearness, into immediacy. Our journey must be to awaken here and now, to awaken *to* here and now. To be fully alive, we must be fully present.

The question is: how do we do it?

In order to experience the answer to this question for yourself, you must come to three realizations. First, you must truly realize that life is fleeting. Next, you must understand that you are already complete, worthy, whole. Finally, you must *see* that you are your own refuge, your own sanctuary, your own salvation.

Pick up a flower—a beautiful, living, fresh rose. It smells wonderful. It reveals a lovely rhythm in the swirl of its petals, a rich yet dazzling color, a soft velvety texture. It moves and delights us.

The problem with the rose is that it dies. Its petals fall; it shrivels up; it turns brown and returns to the earth.

One solution to this problem is to ignore the real rose and substitute a plastic one, one that never dies (and never lives). But is a plastic rose what we want? No, of course not. We want the real rose. We want the one that dies. We want it because it dies, because it's fleeting, because it fades. It's this very quality that makes it precious. This is what we want, what each of us is: a living thing that dies.

Your very own body and mind are also precious, because they're just as fleeting. They're changing—always, in every moment. In fact, you are nothing but change itself.

Let's examine this closely for a moment. It's easy to see that you don't have the body you had when you were a small child. Nor do you have the same mind. If you look carefully, you will notice that you don't even have the same body and mind you had when you turned to this page a few moments ago. In those few seconds, many cells in your body died and many others were created. Countless chemical changes took place in different organs. Your thoughts changed in response to the words on this page and the circumstances around you. Thousands of synapses in your brain fired thousands of times. In each and every moment, you changed.

Like the rose, our bodies and minds are fleeting.

In fact, everything in our experience—our bodies, our minds, our thoughts, our wants and needs, our relationships—is fleeting. Changing. Subject to death. We die in each moment and again, in each moment, we are born. The process of birth and death goes on endlessly, moment after moment, right before our eyes. Everything we look at, including ourselves and every aspect of our lives, is nothing but change.

Vitality consists of this very birth and death. This impermanence, this constant arising and fading away, are the very things that make our lives vibrant, wonderful, and alive.

Yet we usually want to keep things from changing. We want to preserve things, to hold onto them. As we shall see, this desire to hold on, to somehow stop change in its tracks, is the greatest source of woe and horror and trouble in our lives.

You are already in reality, whether you *see* it or not. Reality is what's here, now. Thus you're here now, too. You know all this already, from direct experience. You're not separated from Reality. It's not "out there" somewhere, but right here.

This provides us with the chance to wake up. You have this chance to wake up right now, in this moment, and in every moment. Thus enlightenment is already yours.

Most of us tend to think—and have been taught—that it's the other way around, that we've got to figure something out. But no. We don't need to figure out our own experience; it's already here, firsthand.

You are already enlightened: All you've got to do is stop blocking yourself and get serious about attending to what's going on. You are not lacking a thing. You only need to stop blocking or interpreting your vision.

In his final talk before his death the Buddha said, "Each of you be a light unto yourself; betake yourself to no external refuge. Hold fast to the Truth. Look not for refuge to anyone beside yourself."

You are the final authority. Not me. Not the Buddha. Not the Bible. Not the government. Not the president. Not Mom or Dad. You. No community of philosophers, scientists, priests, academicians, politicians, or generals—no school, legislature, parliament, or court—can bear responsibility for your life, or your words, or your actions. That authority is yours and yours alone. You can neither get rid of it nor escape from it.

Of course, you can pretend to give up this ultimate authority, or ignore it and act as if you haven't got it, or try to give it to someone else. But you haven't really gotten rid of it. *You* gave your authority to someone else. *You* chose to deny or ignore that authority. *You* made the decision to lie to yourself, to pretend that you lack this authority.

Far from being a burden, this ultimate authority is actually quite wonderful. It means that you have the power to wake up. You have it now—in your own hands. You don't have to go anywhere else. You can wake up right now, on the spot. You are fully equipped to do this now, in this moment. You already have all the power you'll ever need to realize happiness.

In other words, you're fully prepared for anything that might come along. Each of us has the power to simply be what we are, with nothing extra added. Nothing's lacking; nothing's missing. You are supported and sustained, right now, even though you may not yet realize it (or realize how). The banquet is spread before you, and you do find nourishment.

To completely end your unease of mind, all you need to do is *see* that there is really nothing "out there" to get because, already, within this moment, everything is whole and complete. In doing so, you can awaken from the perennial confusion, from the existential angst, from the unanswered question of what life is about.

This activity—this *seeing*—is the fourth truth of the buddha-dharma. It is a means by which we can experience freedom of mind.

The buddha-dharma's fourth truth contains eight aspects, which is why it's also called the eightfold path.

Just what is this path? It is, first of all, to *see* what our problem is, and then to resolve to deal with it. In *seeing* you will realize that you must live consciously, not for your sake or someone else's sake or for the sake of some goal or belief or idea, but for the sake of being fully engaged in the moment. Once you *see*, you will speak, act, and maintain your life in a conscious way. Wise speech, action, and livelihood then follow naturally. These provide the foundation for a morality that actually works.

The moral teaching that derives from the buddha-dharma is not a goody-goody code of behavior where we pretend virtue, curry favor, or promise to be good so that we can claim a reward at some later date. Rather, sound morality takes place wholly in the moment. It is based on the immediacy of Reality, on how we actually live. Our "reward" is in immediacy, in here and now, not in a never-never land.

The eightfold path also includes effort, mindfulness, and meditation. But Buddhist meditation is not what many people think of as meditation. It's neither an exercise in relaxation nor a striving toward some special state of mind. This meditation is simply about learning to be here—to be present in each moment and to notice what is going on.

The buddha-dharma does not invite us to dabble in abstract notions. Rather, the task it presents us with is to attend to what we actually experience, right in this moment. You don't have to look "over there." You don't have to figure anything out. You don't have to acquire anything. And you don't have to run off to Tibet, or Japan, or anywhere else. You wake up right here. In fact, you can only wake up right here.

So you don't have to do the long search, the frantic chase, the painful quest. You're already right where you need to be. The table is spread before you. Let's look at how to eat.

2
A Wheel Out of Kilter

The first of the four truths the Buddha described is called *duhkha* (doo-ka). Duhkha is not easily translated into English, so once I've explained it here, I will leave it untranslated. Duhkha is often translated as "suffering." But this only gets at part of what the word means, because pleasure is also a form of duhkha.

In Sanskrit, duhkha stands in opposition to another word, *sukha*, which means "satisfaction." Some people thus translate duhkha as "dissatisfaction." But this doesn't quite hit the mark, either.

Duhkha actually comes from a Sanskrit word that refers to a wheel out of kilter. If we think of this wheel as one that performs some important function, such as a potter's wheel, then the out-of-true wheel creates constant hardship for us every time we try to make a clay vessel.

In the Buddha's time the accompanying image may have been of a cart with an out-of-true wheel being pulled along. You can imagine how uncomfortable it must feel to ride in such a vehicle. The repeated wobble, rise, and drop starts out as annoying, then becomes steadily more distracting and disturbing. Maybe there's a little pleasure in it for the rider at first—a little bounce, perhaps—but after a while it becomes more and more vexing.

The first truth of the buddha-dharma likens human life to this out-of-kilter wheel. Something basic and important isn't right. It bothers us, makes us unhappy, time after time. With each turn of the wheel, each passing day, we experience pain.

Of course there are moments of pleasure. But no matter how hard we try to cultivate pleasure and keep it coming our way, eventually the pleasure recedes and the disturbance and vexation return. Nothing we do can keep them entirely at bay. No matter what we do, our eighty-three problems remain.

What can we do about this? We can begin by seeing clearly and completely just what the problem is.

We've all heard the expression "seeing is believing." But the fact is that believing is not true *seeing*. In fact, they're opposites. Belief is at best an educated, informed conjecture about Reality. In contrast, *seeing*—raw, direct, unadulterated experience—is the direct perception of Reality Itself.

Let's take a quick example. Suppose I were to come up to you, hold out my closed fist, and tell you that I have a jewel in it. Now, I might be lying or I might be telling the truth. Either way, you have little to go on. As long as my hand remains closed you don't know whether or not I have a jewel in it. The most you can do, given the limited information I've provided, is believe or speculate that I have, or don't have, a jewel inside my fist.

Only when I open my fist can you see if there's a jewel in it or not. And once I do open it, the need for—and the usefulness of—belief vanishes. You can see for yourself whether or not there's a jewel, and you can base your actions on what you see, rather than on what you think.

So it is with any issue, question, or dilemma. Belief may serve as a useful stopgap measure in the absence of actual experience, but once you *see* Reality, belief becomes unnecessary. Indeed, at this point, it stands in the way of clear, direct perception. We therefore cannot rely on what we merely believe if we wish to *see* Truth and Reality. We can only rely on actual perception and direct experience.

Truth and Reality (the terms are synonymous) are here for you to *see*. No doo-dads, no knickknacks, no funny hats or secret handshakes. Just Truth itself. Reality itself. Not as you think or hope or believe or imagine, but as it is prior to your (or anyone else's) putting labels on it. This is the only way we can have Truth—by *seeing* it, not by naming it or holding on to it.

Truth or Reality is not something vague, mysterious, or hidden. You don't have to go to someone else to find it—not to a teacher, or a buddha, or your parents, or a priest or rabbi or shaman, or any authority whatsoever. Nor is it something you can look up in a book. Truth comes to us through *seeing*. To *see* is to Know.

Seeing needs no further verification. It's immediate and as one with Truth. But we're usually not very skilled at *seeing* what is actually presented to us.

For a concrete example of what I'm referring to, look at the picture on the next page. Believe it or not, this is a near-photographic rendering of something very familiar, something you've seen (either in person or in pictures) countless times.

If you do not immediately recognize what it is, then notice your state of mind. Notice that it is, to some extent, confused.

Some people, when they first see this picture, say, "I think it might be a man lying down." But they say it with uncertainty. They're not quite sure. They believe it might be a man reclining. (That's what I thought when I first saw the picture.) But there's no sense of seeing, no conviction that you know what the picture depicts.

Keep looking at the picture. I assure you that when you actually see what it is, all your uncertainty will immediately vanish. You will know what the picture is. All beliefs and uneasiness about it will instantly cease.

If you haven't yet seen what this picture is, keep looking at it for a while. Eventually you'll get it. And when you do get it, notice the sudden shift that takes place in your mind. (If it begins to seem hopeless and you need help, you'll find the solution in the text on page 154. But try to hold out until you do see what

MYSTERIOUS FIGURE

it is, so you can witness the shock of recognition and the pro-found shift in your mind.)

Did you notice how your mind relaxed when, suddenly, you saw, and knew you saw? Your state of mind, which before was vague, mysterious, fuzzy, confused, and uncomfortable, was sud-denly transformed the moment you saw. You had clarity and total conviction. And that clarity and conviction will remain with you each time you view this picture again. If somebody says to you, "It's a picture of a man lying down," you'll know they're off the mark—and no amount of argument is going to influence you.

This is analogous to the difference between *seeing* and simply having a belief, an idea, a concept.

The buddha-dharma points the way to a similar, but more universal and profound, sense of "Aha!" It's not about pondering some vague, faraway realm. It's about here and now. About wak-ing up to this moment, *seeing this* for what it is. And, just as your state of mind changed once you saw what the picture was, when you suddenly *see* the situation you're in, you experience certainty. Things clear up.

This is called enlightenment, or awakening.

This awakening is available to all of us, at every moment, with-out exception.

As long as we remain in our common state of confusion, however, our minds are characterized by vexation, by duhkha. In fact, if we look carefully and seriously at our situation, we'll *see* that we experience three kinds of duhkha.

The first kind of duhkha is straightforward pain, both physi-cal and mental. Whether we like it or not, pain is an unavoidable part of our lives. We can dampen it, medicate or anesthetize ourselves against it, take steps to avoid or minimize it, and sometimes we succeed in reducing it. But we cannot entirely escape it. Sooner or later, even if you're perfectly healthy now, you'll get injured, you'll be sick, you'll hurt, you'll die.

In fact, in many cases our attempts to limit or avoid pain can actually increase our suffering. The classic example is the fellow with a toothache who puts off going to the dentist because he's afraid that the treatment will hurt. Because he delays too long, he develops a serious infection and needs a root canal—a much more painful, time-consuming, and expensive treatment than he'd have needed if he had seen a dentist promptly.

Physical suffering occurs whenever something is out of kilter in our bodies. Mental suffering arises whenever we feel something is out of kilter in our lives, in others' lives, or in the world in general. Mental suffering takes place when we don't get what we want, or when we're forced to live with and endure what we don't want.

The fact is that we can't really turn our heads away from pain. Wherever we turn, it's with us. We have to face it or we are never going to find our way out of the situation we are in—this situation of duhkha. We can only deal with pain by facing it squarely.

The second form of duhkha is change. All aspects of our experience, both physical and mental, are in constant flux and change.

Whatever we think, whatever we can point to or look at or talk about, is in constant flux. If we are in our ordinary state of mind, as opposed to an awakened state, this flux registers as dissatisfaction, disturbance, duhkha.

And then we magnify our problem by longing (and trying) to stop that change, to fix things in their places. We attempt this externally through force, control, and manipulation. And we attempt it internally as well, by conceptualizing the world. We try to nail everything down, arrange everything in our minds so that we are left with a sense of meaning or purpose or relief.

Even if we manage to make our situation comfortable for the moment, it can only be temporary. All circumstances surrounding this momentary situation will inevitably change. And when they do, our momentary pleasure will depart, only to reveal duhkha once again.

This attempt to nail down the world is a profound, if subtle, manifestation of the second form of duhkha. It is so painful and disturbing because it's nothing more than our desperate attempt to defy Reality. We may long for an other-worldly abode, a place where such pain and vexation will never strike. We may even try to create such a place, internally or externally. But no such place exists, or ever has, or ever can. A moment of reflection on death should make this obvious. Everything that lives must die; everything that comes into being must come to an end or change its form. It is simply impossible for anything to exist and not change.

So long as we remain in our ordinary state of mind, there's no escape from the inevitable duhkha brought about by change. But we tend not to look at this. Instead, we generally try to control and manipulate the world: our lives, our relationships, events, other people. This attempt is the single greatest source of the second type of duhkha.

Until we *see* that this is so, our highest priority will still be to get in there and control and manipulate. We'll honestly believe that in doing so we can make the world better for ourselves and for everyone else. We won't realize that all we create in this process is havoc—pain, vexation, and mental and physical distress: duhkha.

Our way out is not through control or intentional action, but through *seeing*. *Just seeing* is enough. But how and what to *see?* We'll come to this shortly.

Beyond the duhkha of pain, beyond the duhkha of change, is the duhkha of being. This third form of duhkha is much harder to *see* than the first two. It usually requires some serious contemplation.

As long as you see yourself as a distinct, separate entity, you must also see yourself as subject to death. If your existence is in being, then you must inevitably pass out of existence. This realization carries with it profound pain, distress, or horror.

The simplest way to experience this form of duhkha is just to sit quietly and reflect on the fact that you do not know the answers to some very basic questions. How did you get here? What are you? Where did you come from? Where are you going? You may have beliefs and ideas about these questions, but you do not know the answers to any of them through your own direct experience.

Look at how vast the world is. Is there some purpose to all of it? Look how insignificant each one of us is against this vastness. What is human life for? Why does any of this exist at all? Why is there something rather than nothing?

And then there's the big, unanswered question: "What will happen to me after I die?" We have all sorts of stories about heaven and hell, about oblivion and nothingness, about "coming back," and so on. But they are all stories. The teaching of the awakened is not about telling ourselves a story. It is about investigating actual experience. What does actual experience say about the big question? Can we understand anything about where we came from, or where we're going, or why we're here, or what will happen to each of us when we die? Yes, we can. But we cannot get any satisfaction by trying to figure out the answers to such questions.

However, if you scrutinize your own experience carefully, this profound unease we all experience just by existing can vanish— just as that uneasy state of mind vanished once you saw what was in that mysterious figure on page 30. Through *seeing* you can Know.

3

Coming

The second truth of the buddha-dharma is the arising of duhkha. Duhkha arises from thirst—craving, wanting, trying to get the object of our desire into our hands. This craving or wanting appears in three different forms.

First there is sensual desire. We tend to think that this is purely physical, but it is also mental. Of course, we want comfortable, yet stimulating, physical sensations, but we also want good intellectual stimulation: good conversation, a balanced emotional life, enjoyable art and entertainment, and so on. Our sensual craving is, in fact, mostly mental.

Our second form of craving is our thirst for existence itself. We don't want to die. We want to somehow persist, live on, forever.

But even if we could abandon our thirst for existence, there's still a third form of craving that plagues us: the thirst for nonexistence. We want to be released from this world of pain and vexation once and for all.

Duhkha arises repeatedly in our hearts and minds as these three forms of craving. When we don't realize that this is so, we forget this moment and get caught up in longing and loathing—desiring some things to come (or stay) and others to go.

Virtually all the woes of humankind stem from these three forms of craving. Our greatest pains are thus all self-inflicted. Name what afflicts you and you will ultimately find it linked to your craving, your wanting, your desiring.

But we tend not to notice this. Basically, we're confused about what we actually want. We don't easily *see* that all we really want—all any of us want—is simply to be awake. We don't want to be confused. We don't want to go through life in a state of ignorance. But generally we're ignorant even of this.

Because we ignore this deep need of the heart, we seek to appease our desire by acquiring and blocking out. We fancy that some combination of money and fame and love and lack of stress will drive away all our woes. But nothing that can be acquired ever does . . . and we know it.

The awakened do not promise that our eighty-three problems—the vicissitudes of daily life—will go away. No, the ups and downs of life remain with life. But in dealing with the eighty-fourth problem—in *seeing* the arising of duhkha—our problems are not exactly problems anymore.

My Zen teacher used to tell the story of a fellow who wanted out—not out of life, just out of the Zen monastery where he was living.

In Zen monasteries you must pay constant attention to what you're doing, what you're experiencing from moment to moment. All your activities are prescribed, and they're carried out in deliberate stillness. After a time, this can get to you—which is precisely what happened to the fellow in this story. He went to see the master and said, "I can't take this anymore. I want out."

The master said, "Okay, then leave."

As he started for the door the teacher said, "That's not your door."

"Oh! Sorry." The startled fellow looked around and spotted a second door. As he headed for it the teacher said, "That's not your door."

"Oh!" He looked around for another door. He could see that behind the teacher was a little door normally used by the teacher's attendant. As he headed for that door the teacher screamed at him, "That's not your door!"

Totally bewildered and exasperated, the poor fellow said, "What do you mean? There's no other door! You told me I could leave, but there's no door I can leave by!"

"If there's no door you can leave by," said the teacher, "then sit down."

We can only be here. We can't leave. We're always here. Examine your life and you'll *see* that this is the case.

The master's "sit down" means to start paying attention to what's actually going on, instead of running away from it. This is the only way we'll put an end to our underlying pain and confusion.

Unfortunately, we try to deal with most of our problems by heading for the door, by trying to leave our immediate situation by any means we can. But our real problem—the deep-down ache of the heart—doesn't go anywhere. It travels with us. This deep-down problem is confusion.

Our most painful problems—war, crime, poverty, ignorance, greed, degradation—are not natural disasters. Which makes you more sick at heart, the Los Angeles earthquake or the Los Angeles riots? Bad as an earthquake is, it's in such moments that people come together and help each other. Amid the smoke and rubble, people reach out to one another and become more trusting in the process.

But while there are always a few noble actions taken by some heroic individuals in the midst of a riot, the source of any riot is always us—human beings. The conditions that create it are us. The igniting of it is us. The doing of it is us. And the continuing of it is us. Unlike an earthquake, a riot is totally a result of our power—which means it's totally within our power to prevent.

But in order to prevent it, we must first face our true situation.

Ignorance can be insidious if we're not careful. Consider how, even in getting the wonderful things we long for, we tend to live in want of something more, of whatever might come to us next. This can only go on for so long before life becomes meaningless. Either that or we're regularly frustrated by not getting what we want. Henry Ford, after he made his first billion dollars, was asked how much more he wanted. He said he wanted just a little more.

This is how it is with us. Because we ignore our true situation, we're set up to never be satisfied. We're like the comic strip character Hagar the Horrible who, when asked which he'd choose, power, gold, or true happiness, chose power: "With power, I could get the gold, and then I'd be happy."

We find Hagar's idea humorous because we know better. Yet most of the time we ignore this very knowledge, and act (or at least think) much like Hagar.

Good times come and go. And bad times do the same. Still, we spend much of our time and energy trying to get the good times back. We fail to notice that the good time arrives of its own. Likewise the bad times appear even though we spend much time and energy trying to keep it at bay.

We don't want bad times, of course. But bad times are out of our control as much as good times. The times we don't want will come (and go) no matter what we do to control the situation. The good times will do the same. Thus, beyond just simply living fully in each moment, we should realize that such control is impossible, a pipe dream.

This doesn't mean we shouldn't set things up for the future. It does mean that we would do well not to become attached to particular outcomes. We'd do better focusing our effort on being present rather than on insisting on what the future must be.

Breaking the grip of ignorance and craving comes with *just seeing*, not with doing something particular about it. Once you *see*, your course of action will naturally follow.

The problem in dealing with craving is that when we try to squelch it, we only step it up somewhere else. It comes bursting out more intensely than ever. For example, suppose you notice, "I'm craving a pizza now." That's fine. Just notice it.

But we usually don't stop there. Rather than *just seeing*, we act upon what we notice instead: "I shouldn't be wanting pizza. I must stop this desire for pizza."

This very reaction is already more craving. We're desiring an end to desire. We're doing the usual thing again—reaching for, insisting, grabbing. This is bondage, not freedom. This is a subtle but crucial point. There's no bandage to use on this problem that will not itself be the same problem all over again.

The only way to eradicate this problem is to *see* it and thereby no longer feed it.

This is not a call to complacency or inaction. To act or not to act is never the question. You can't help but act. The question is whether or not you *see*. The entire issue rests on this.

This issue, of course, is hard enough to *see* clearly even after it's been pointed out to us. As we live our lives it's harder still to *see*—yet this is where it counts.

Our problem comes from what the Buddha described as "inclination of mind." The mind tends to lean in one direction or another because, out of ignorance, it sees something "out there" which it then craves. "I want that back," "I want that now," or "I don't want that anymore. Push it away, get rid of it." Either way, we define what we want or don't want as something separate from us.

In the enlightened mind, the mind of a buddha, there's no such inclination, no such leaning. On the other hand, our ordinary mind—our conceptual mind—does lean. It's full of picki choosing, of wanting and craving. Seng-ts'an, one of the f ers of Zen Buddhism in China, wrote in "Trusting the F mind" that picking and choosing is the mind's worst disease. The Germans have an expression, "Whoever has choice, has torment." It's true. Wherever choice appears, the mind is immediately put ill at ease.

Duhkha—suffering, pain—is associated with choice. The more we fail to understand this, the more we'll be caught up in duhkha. And the more we'll not *see* the subtlety of it.

We live in a culture where we're taught to see freedom as the maximization of choice. But this is not true freedom at all. In fact, it's a form of bondage. True freedom doesn't lie in the maximization of choice, but, ironically, is most easily found in a life where there is little choice.

Consider this: often the more serious the choice, the easier it becomes to make it.

I realized this when I had cancer. My doctor wanted to give me chemotherapy, but I was averse to even taking aspirin. The thought of putting those powerful chemicals in my body repelled me thoroughly. Yet I had a massive tumor in my chest, lumps in my neck, tumors in my abdomen. I was underweight and very weak and tired. Without treatment, I had only a few weeks to live, but there was a slim chance that I could survive a few months, perhaps even a year or more, with the treatments.

Though I was repulsed by the thought, the choice was easy. I said yes to the chemotherapy. That was nearly twenty years ago.

This is not to say that freedom of mind is about giving up choice. Choices will always remain in the shifting details and circumstances of our lives. But the fact is, when it comes to freedom of mind, choice is easy. We have no choice but to wake up.

When petty choices occupy the mind necessity is forgotten, and wanting and craving, picking and choosing take over. The mind is ill at ease and dissatisfied for want of the next petty thing. Life and death choices are few and (usually) easy to make, painful as they may be. Inconsequential choices are not, yet we needlessly clutter our lives with them. We think they bring pleasure, but they only breed dissatisfaction.

Thus, without realizing what we're actually doing to ourselves, we become ever more bound.

If we're not careful, we make our lives busy, complicated, and unnecessary. We fill ourselves with a sense of vacancy and meaninglessness. Our minds become complicated by petty details and wants, and we become ever more confused. But in our quiet moments, we sense that no freedom lies in maximizing petty choices. It's the wrong game plan . . . and we know it.

Let's consider another way intention is joined with duhkha.

In my youth I drove an Austin Healey Sprite, a little sports car, much like an MG. It was a rag-top, a soft-top convertible.

On one occasion I took a trip across the country with a friend. To save money we camped along the way. It was March, the off-season. We arrived late one night at the Indiana Dunes State Park along the shore of Lake Michigan. I thought it might be closed, but the gate was open when we got there. No one was around, so we drove straight to the camping area to set up the tent. We were tired from traveling, so we turned in as soon as we were set.

Before I retired I took off my watch and hung it on the turn signal stem in my car. Since no one was around, I also put my wallet on the dash. Then I crawled into my sleeping bag and went to sleep.

My friend was entirely unfamiliar with sleeping in a tent. After I had slept a while, he woke me. He was disturbed by something moving around outside. He was a city kid; he thought it might be a burglar. I laughed it off. I was used to camping, and I expected critters to rustle around the tent at night. I told him not to worry, rolled over, and went back to sleep.

The next day, when I stepped outside the tent, I stood next to my car to take my morning stretch. As I stood there with my arms spread wide, I realized that the roof of my car had been slashed in a T, allowing the sides to fall in around a big, gaping hole.

It appeared to be a wanton act of destruction, for my wallet was still on the dash, and my watch was still on the turn signal. It was just slash and run. I felt terrible. Who would just slash my roof with a knife for no reason? I didn't want to live in a world where people did this sort of thing.

Later, as I walked through the woods nearby, I came upon a shredded box of cookies. There were no cookies, just the remains of the box. I didn't think anything of it but threw it in the trash.

A while later, back in the car, my friend started poking around in the open compartment in front of the passenger seat. Suddenly he burst out, "Hey! My cookies are gone!"

It all came together in a flash: my friend from the city had been innocent enough to leave a box of cookies in the car overnight, and a raccoon had slashed my roof in order to get at them.

Immediately my bad feeling about the incident changed. When I thought my slashed roof was the wanton act of a person, I felt a sickness in my heart that went beyond mere irritation at having a slashed roof. But when I realized it was a raccoon . . . well, of course, a raccoon isn't going to think, "Those aren't my cookies. I shouldn't eat them." A raccoon just enters the only way he knows how, with no sense of malice or ownership. There was food, and naturally he helped himself. There was no confusion, no blame.

Suddenly I no longer felt any great suffering. There was no more of that hollow, unbearable ache of the heart.

But why should my mental state alter so drastically with this realization? Why is the raccoon's action so different from that of a vandal?

The difference is intention.

We often think the purpose of taking up a spiritual practice is to produce good actions as opposed to bad. According to the buddha-dharma, however, this is completely beside the point. The point is, rather, that we become aware of when and how we act out of our intent.

Most of us, most of the time, tend to act with intent, trying to bring about some desired end. But nature doesn't act with intent. A buddha doesn't either. Acting without intent means acting out of Wholeness—out of *seeing* the Whole.

But why not just learn to do good as opposed to bad?

Because no solid, unchanging "good" or "bad" can be established. Good and bad aren't absolutes. They are beliefs, judgments, ideas based on limited knowledge as well as on the inclinations of our minds.

The situation we always live in is like that of the wise Chinese farmer whose horse ran off. When his neighbor came to console him the farmer said, "Who knows what's good or bad?"

When his horse returned the next day with a herd of horses following her, the foolish neighbor came to congratulate him on his good fortune.

"Who knows what's good or bad?" said the farmer.

Then, when the farmer's son broke his leg trying to ride one of the new horses, the foolish neighbor came to console him again.

"Who knows what's good or bad?" said the farmer.

When the army passed through, conscripting men for war, they passed over the farmer's son because of his broken leg. When the foolish man came to congratulate the farmer that his son would be spared, again the farmer said, "Who knows what's good or bad?"

When do we expect the story to end?

Socrates pointed out that we carry on as though death were the greatest of all calamities—yet, for all we know, it might be the greatest of all blessings. What are we going to call good? What are we going to call bad? Good or bad is never our choice, or even the issue.

During the Civil War, both sides claimed the support of God. It was clear to each side that they were doing the righteous thing.

PART ONE: THE PERENNIAL PROBLEM

Such sentiments were voiced often enough for President Lincoln to observe, "God cannot be for and against the same thing at the same time."

We'll only make ourselves ever more deluded the longer we play this game. Good versus bad is clearly not the issue. There's something more fundamental at stake.

But what do we look for?

If your idea of good opposes something else, you can be sure that what you call "good" is not absolute or certain. It's only in *seeing* that we can hope to find what lies beyond our shaky, relative ideas of good and bad. If we would live in a way that is somehow beyond the uncertain dualities of the relative world, we must learn to observe our inclination of mind—our intention, our will, our thirsting desire.

Don't squelch your desire, or try to stop it. You'll only feed and intensify it. The point is not to kill desire. The point is to *see*.

4

Going

The buddha-dharma's third truth simply states that whatever is subject to arising is also subject to ceasing. And since duhkha arises, it too is subject to cessation.

The cessation of duhkha—the ending of confusion, sorrow, and loss—is nirvana.

The Buddha referred to nirvana as "unborn, ungrown, and unconditioned." He said,

> Were there not the unborn, ungrown, and uncondi-
> tioned, there would be no escape for the born, grown,
> and conditioned. Since there is the unborn, ungrown,
> and unconditioned, so there is escape for the born,
> grown, and conditioned.

The born, grown, and conditioned refer to everything you can conceive of—including yourself.

Look around you. There's nothing you can find—indeed, there's nothing you can even imagine—that doesn't originate, develop, or exist in relation to other things. Being born, growing, and responding to conditions is built into the very fabric of the world we live in.

But the Buddha also pointed out that there is an aspect of experience that is not born, grown, or conditioned. This unconditioned aspect is directly available to perception. We can *see* it—we just can't conceptualize it or pin it down.

In short, our situation is anything but hopeless. There actually is something Real, Genuine, and True for us to *see*.

Back when I had cancer, I would occasionally meet with others who had cancer. We always had much to share. And so it happened that I became friends with a man who was dying of the illness.

I used to visit him in the hospital. But I remember one evening in particular when everything seemed different. It wasn't like the other nights I had visited him. For one thing, the hospital seemed so much quieter than usual.

My friend was lying in bed, hooked up to a machine that would sigh on occasion and break the silence every few minutes. Otherwise it was extremely quiet, except for the radio, tuned to the classical station, which was barely audible.

I sat by his bed and we talked quietly for a while. Our conversation was mostly silence. Just the radio and the sighing machine.

He was in pain and asked me to give him a massage. I did for a few minutes. Then, again, we talked for a while.

After a silence, he suddenly put his hands over his face and gave out a forceful gasp. Reality was overtaking him at last. He had been struggling with cancer for the better part of a year, but in that moment, the reality of his death was finally hitting him. At last he put his hands down and just stared ahead.

I said to him, "Wherever we go, it's always like this."

Puzzled, he looked at me and said, "What do you mean?"

I gestured and said, "*thus.*"

The look of bewilderment remained for a moment. Then his face transformed. He understood.

It was the last time we spoke to each other.

I sat with him a while longer, in that deathly silent room with the gasping machine. And the radio, exceedingly soft.

He died the next day.

Some people think the teaching of the awakened is nihilistic, as if it asserts a kind of nothingness. As if, somehow, nirvana is a lapsing into a tranquil oblivion, a floating grayness, drifting in a shoreless sea. That is not nirvana.

Recall that everything we see, hear, feel, and think is constant flux and change. Nothing endures. We long for permanence and as a result we suffer, for we find none. There seems to be only this coming and going, coming and going, this unending arising and ceasing.

We experience everything as motion. Indeed, physicists tell us that matter is literally nothing but motion. And no matter how we look at it, at any scale, our experience is always of motion, of change.

This is true of everything in the physical world, including our bodies. Every cell—indeed, every atom of every cell—reveals nothing but ceaseless coming and going. Our bodies are re-made moment by moment, and in no two moments are they the same.

The same is true of our minds. The contents of our minds are in constant motion as well. Thoughts, feelings, judgments, and impulses arise, one after another, then bloom and fade away like flowers after their season.

Nirvana is *seeing*, thoroughly and completely, that this is so.

We need to see our situation for what it is. We're not really crazy or stupid. We just don't see—that is, we don't pay attention to what we see.

We tend to think of ourselves as persons or individuals—separate entities persisting through time.

But we aren't.

What we call a person, the Buddha referred to simply as "stream."

If you're like most people, you think of yourself as having been born. But if you look at this notion carefully, you'll see that you have no immediate experience of having come into existence at all. Trace it back. Follow your memory. Do you remember coming into existence?

Of course, you didn't begin at birth—but when did you begin? At conception? When, exactly, does conception take place? When the sperm first finds the egg?

But what about that sperm and egg? When did they begin? With your parents? And when did they begin? And their parents before them?

The truth is that you can't find "coming into being" as an event in actual experience. Everything involves what came before it in its identity. It's dependent on earlier conditions which, in turn, are dependent on earlier conditions still, and so on as far back as we can trace or imagine. In other words, there's something very odd and contradictory and unsettling about this concept of "coming into being."

Nevertheless, here's Reality. Here's the world. Here's *thus*.

This same problem occurs with anything conceivable. For example, I'm sitting here at my computer writing these words. But when did these words become a book? As I wrote them? When I finished the final edit? When I gave the manuscript to my publisher? When the printed pages were bound?

When did this book begin? When I first conceived of writing it? Yet this book has evolved over decades. Did it begin when I first began studying Buddhism? When the insights it's based on were first taught twenty-five centuries ago? The fact is, the writing of this book is inseparable from the efforts and insights of countless people over millennia.

And what about endings? Where does this book (or you, or I) end? If all is flux, then there is no persistent thing such as a book (or you, or I) that can come to an end. The material that makes up this book in this one particular moment is going through—has always gone through—endless transformations, giving no indication that such transformations will ever cease.

And if we say that the essence of this book (or you, or I) resides not in materiality but in its mental or intellectual dimensions, again we find only endless transformations, with nothing being created or destroyed.

We have stories that say "In the beginning God created . . ." But then, where did God come from?

If all is truly flux, where do we find beginnings or endings? We're like the foolish neighbor who keeps going to the wise farmer to alternately console and congratulate him. When do we expect the story to end?

Both the beginning and the end are inconceivable.

Let's look again at the three desires we discussed in the last chapter, but this time from a different angle.

The first, the desire for sensory pleasure, can be seen as simply the desire to please ourselves. We just want to be happy. But how can you be truly happy when you've got a death sentence on your head?

This brings us to the second desire. We'd prefer not to die. How are you going to get around that one? If you were born, you're going to die. It's as simple as that. But what if this view of extinction, which has such a profound grip on us, turns out not to be correct? What if it is actually founded in confusion? And if it is, how can we know this and thus free ourselves from such a view?

Our problem is that we don't *see* change as mere coming and going. Instead, we think that it somehow entails persistence—even though this is in contradiction to direct experience, which reveals only flux and change. We imagine that things come into existence, endure for a while, and then pass out of existence.

Because we think this way, we have yet another desire: the desire for non-existence—the desire to control our extinction.

All three of these desires arise because of our confusion about change.

The Buddha talked of extinguishing these desires. But how can we do that? Isn't our very intention to do so just another desire? And doesn't one desire lead to another? It would seem that desires are inexhaustible. So what are we to do?

We can stop feeding the flame of desire, and let that flame diminish and go out, like a lamp that has burned all its fuel.

The buddha-dharma offers us two ways of doing this. The first is what the Buddha called "less desire." The second is often called "forgetting the self."

It is said that if you drop a frog in hot water, he'll jump out. If you put him in lukewarm water and very slowly raise the temperature, the frog will stay there until he dies.

We're not frogs. We have the capacity to *see* and to *know* when we're sliding too far into an unhealthy situation. But we have to take note of what we *see*. We don't have to continue down a slippery slope. We can stop, turn around, and head in the other direction. But this can only be done when we *see* our situation for what it is.

This backing away from the precipice is the practice of less desire.

Our senses numb when we overload them. But once they're numb, it's tempting to overload them even more until we're too numb to feel much at all. This is precisely the vicious cycle of an addictive drug. The overall effect we experience is the opposite of what we desired.

But it's not merely drugs that are addictive and have the power to take us over the edge. For example, as the millennium draws to a close, we've become jaded about great art and music simply because, with our technology, we've made it all too commonplace. When we can see reproductions of van Gogh's *Sunflowers* regularly, we no longer see their incredible, screaming vitality. And how much power is left in Beethoven's Fifth Symphony after the hundredth hearing? (It might help to remember that for the people of Beethoven's day, just hearing it at all would be a rare event.)

How can we deal with this situation? Should we attempt to snuff out our desires? Should we think of our desires as nasty, or wrong, or evil? Of course not. Those approaches simply add more fuel to the same fire.

So what can we do? First we *see.* Then we turn and gently go back.

There's no pressure we need to put on ourselves. Simply by *seeing* how things actually are—what leads to confusion and what leads to clarity—we begin to turn around.

Nature has its checks and balances. We tend to override them with our thoughts. We can, however, make a conscious effort to *see*, and let the balance restore itself. With *seeing*, restoring balance is no more problematic and sacrificial than not putting our hand in a flame. When we *see* what the act entails, we just don't have the urge to do it anymore.

The other way to deal with our desires is to direct the focus of our desires away from ourselves. To forget the self is to remember that we don't exist alone, but in relation to other people, to other creatures, to the planet, and to the universe. It is to focus not on ourselves as a force in charge of the manipulation of others, but on how our lives interpenetrate those of others—and, indeed, all the activities of a dynamic universe.

Thus we have endless opportunities to forget the self—in planting a tree for future generations; in creating a poem, a meal, a vessel of clay; in playing baseball, wholeheartedly, knowing that your opponents are as vital to the game as you are.

Generally our desire, our actions, our speech, and our thoughts are geared toward bringing about some particular end by exerting control. Then, when these efforts at control fail (as they inevitably must if held onto too long), we suffer.

The buddha-dharma doesn't ask us to give up control. Instead, it acknowledges that we never had it in the first place. When we can see this, the desire to control naturally begins to wane. The point is not to try to stop exerting control, or to condemn the desire to control as bad or wrong. The point is to *see* things as they are, to acknowledge what's really going on. Through such acknowledgment and recognition, we can cease to suffer.

At the center of our desire for control is our sense of self. But with seeing, this sense loses its grip. What becomes extinguished is this false sense of self. We stop clinging to something that wasn't there to begin with.

Our first reaction to this might be, "But who would want that?" If we look at this more carefully we'll find profound liberation in it. For if what frightens us most is in fact illusory, then waking up to its illusory nature yields the most profound freedom. Our greatest fear is that each of us—"I"—will someday pass out of existence. But how can something cease to exist that had no solid existence in the first place?

The Buddha said,

> Just as a man shudders with horror when he steps upon a serpent, but laughs when he looks down and sees that it is only a rope, so I discovered one day that what I was calling "I" cannot be found, and all fear and anxiety vanished with my mistake.

The buddha-dharma points the way for each of us to wake up from this same basic mistake. And when we awaken, our fears and anxieties quite naturally vanish, as the night fades away at the rising of the sun.

5

The Art of Seeing

The fourth truth of the buddha-dharma, also known as the eightfold path, offers us a realization and a practice for bringing about the cessation of duhkha.

This is not a path we can take to get from point A to point B. Its peculiar nature is that the moment we step on it, the entire path is realized at once. Still, with each step we take we can deepen our understanding.

The eight aspects of this path are *right view, right intention, right speech, right action, right livelihood, right effort, right mindfulness,* and *right meditation.*

We'll preview each of these in a moment, but first let's consider the word "right." The word the Buddha actually used was *samma.* *Samma* is usually translated as "right"—but not "right" as opposed to "wrong," or "bad," or "evil." Normally, the moment we say "right," we've already implied "wrong." We've implied dualism.

For those unfamiliar with the term as it's being used here, dualism simply refers to the world of left and right, dark and light, good and bad, pure and impure. It's the psychological backdrop for our everyday world of chasing after some things and running away from others, the world in which if you differ from me, then there's something wrong with you.

Obviously, this isn't what the Buddha meant by *samma*. The term suggests something far more subtle. It's better that we understand right as "this is appropriate," "this works," "this is in sync with Reality." Right, on the eightfold path, doesn't mean right versus wrong so much as it means *seeing* versus *not seeing*. It refers to being in touch with Reality as opposed to being deluded by our own prejudices, thoughts, and beliefs. *Samma* refers to Wholeness rather than fragmentation.

Thus, when I use the word "right" in the chapters to come, I intend it to refer to what is conducive to awakening, rather than something that can be compared against something wrong.

The first aspect of the eightfold path is *right view*. According to the Buddha, to hold onto any particular view is to freeze Reality, to try to encapsulate the world into thought. To take a view is like taking a snapshot—you've frozen the scene right there.

Once we hold a view, it's not long before our view will buck up against other views. After that, the people holding the various views will file off into separate camps. And then we start to go after each other.

What the Buddha meant by *right view* isn't like this at all. The *view* of a buddha isn't an ordinary, frozen view.

There are those who argue that the Buddha didn't have any view whatsoever, but this is not correct. What the Buddha meant by *right view* is not being caught by a particular view. It's not being caught by ideas, concepts, beliefs, or opinions.

The *view* of a buddha is of how things actually are—which, in light of the constant flux and flow of the world, is no one way in particular. After all, how can things be a particular way if they are in constant motion? How can a hard-and-fast view of a world that is never hard or fast possibly be accurate?

It's not the particulars of the world that provide us with *right view*, but the world itself, as an ever-dynamic Whole. *Right view* is Wholesome—that is, it's of the Whole. It's all-inclusive. It leaves nothing out. Such a view, by definition, does not go to war with any other view. In fact, it cannot. Since it's already of the dynamic world as a Whole, we can't conceive of anything that opposes it.

The second aspect of the Path is *right intention*. It's also sometimes called *right resolve*, *right motive*, or *right thought*.

There's a story of Socrates testing the true intent of a youth who came to him for instruction. He wanted to see if this young man had the resolve to search for Truth. He took the youth to the river, and, after wading into the water, asked the young man to follow. Once they were waist-deep, Socrates suddenly took hold of the fellow and held him under the water. Naturally, the youth soon began to struggle for air. Socrates then lifted him from the water and said, "When you fight for truth as you fight for breath, come back and I'll teach you."

This is *right intention, right resolve.*

You cannot actually learn Truth from anyone. It's *seen* only through your own resolve. If you do not resolve to awaken, there's nothing a teacher can do for you. *Right resolve* is likened to a person whose hair is on fire. When your hair is on fire, you're not going to weigh the pros and cons of putting it out. If your hair's on fire, there's no waffling. You *see* no choice. You act.

Right speech is the next aspect of the eightfold path.

The most obvious form of *right speech* is avoiding lying. Whatever moral justification you may have for not lying, there are some very practical reasons for being truthful. The eightfold path is to keep your mind from becoming too disturbed, so that you can remain present here and now. (After all, it's only *here* and *now* that you awaken.) If you were to lie, your mind would be immediately distracted. Now you have to keep track of what you said, and to whom, and how the story should progress, and so on. There's no end. Waking up suddenly becomes more difficult.

A second factor of *right speech* is not speaking crudely or rudely. Such speech is unnecessary, undignified, and disturbing.

Other aspects of *right speech* include not speaking ill of others and refraining from gossip and idle talk. Obviously, wallowing in triviality, slander, or fantasy is not conducive to waking up.

The fourth aspect of the eightfold path is *right action*. This is action that proceeds from an unfettered mind, a mind not embalmed in rigid thought constructs.

Aspect five of the eightfold path is *right livelihood*. How are we to earn our keep on this planet without doing violence to others, to the environment, or to ourselves?

The buddha-dharma does not provide lists of approved professions, of course; rather, it offers guidance to help each of us wake up to how we may earn a living that encourages openness, insight, honesty, and harmony.

Right effort, the sixth aspect of the eightfold path, is a conscious and ongoing engagement with each moment. It's the willing abandonment of our fragmented mentality and dualistic thought, moment after moment, and the encouragement of healthy and Wholesome states of mind.

Right effort is closely associated with the seventh aspect of the eightfold path, *right mindfulness*. This simply means not forgetting what our real problem is: duhkha.

Through *right mindfulness*, we acquaint and regularly reacquaint ourselves with the states and functions of our own minds, with how we are actually engaged in the world from moment to moment. Through this observation and awareness we can become intimate with how we operate out of each of these mental states.

The final aspect of the eightfold path is *right meditation* or *right concentration*. *Right meditation* is collecting the mind so that it becomes focused, centered, and aware. Chapter Eight will provide a basic introduction to this simple form of meditation.

Please do not take any of these aspects of the eightfold path on faith. Test them out. Engage them in your own life and see for yourself whether or not they are conducive to awakening. Remember: the buddha-dharma is about *seeing*, not about believing.

Closely associated with the eightfold path is a series of general guidelines for living called the Buddhist precepts. These precepts are not rules. They are sometimes compared to the Ten Commandments because they often appear as a list of ten. But they're not commandments, or even rules at all. They simply have to do with how to live in immediate Reality, without indulging in whims and fancies, likes and dislikes. Instead of prescribing specific actions or activities, these precepts encourage us to live by *seeing*, by being awake in each moment.

If you were to attempt strictly to follow a moral rule, before long you'd be in real confusion because you would come up against a variety of contradictions and paradoxes. Real moral responsibility lies in being awake in each moment. This necessarily leaves hard and fast rules behind.

For example, suppose you're harboring a family of Jews in your attic when two Gestapo officers come to your door. They ask you the whereabouts of the family. Do you say they're in your attic?

In these circumstances, the wisest and most compassionate course of action will very likely be to lie. Yet if you felt compelled to follow an absolute rule—"Thou shalt not lie"—then you'd have to say, "Oh, they're upstairs."

On the other hand, if you're not bound by a rule, you can tell the Gestapo the family has gone to Ontario to visit relatives.

This doesn't mean that lying is generally the thing to do, of course. It means that to be moral you must observe the actual situation as well as your own cast of mind. What is moral is that which is most conducive to waking up. This is what the precepts are all about.

If you throw your moral circumstance into a conceptual form by applying some rigid formulation, you're immediately in trouble. By *seeing* the situation as it is, you are able to act out of Reality, not out of some mental formulation of it.

There's no rule in the end, but only the situation and the inclination of your own mind.

Part Two

THE WAY TO WAKE UP

6
Wisdom

Seeker: "Teach me the way to liberation."
Zen master: "Who binds you?"
Seeker: "No one binds me."
Zen master: "Then why seek liberation?"

Our prison, our dungeon, is in us. It's in our own mind, our own thinking. We strap ourselves in chains of our own making, and we do the same to each other. We train our children in the ways of bondage.

All this is based on ignorance. We don't *see* what we are. We don't *see* our situation for what it is, nor do we *see* how to deal with it. As Yang Chu says, we pass by the joys of life without knowing we've missed anything.

Ordinarily, when you step on a path, you're going somewhere. You start on it, traverse it, and, if all goes as planned, you arrive at your goal or destination.

The path to freeing the mind is not like this. This path neither begins nor ends. Thus it's not really a path to somewhere.

Furthermore, the moment you set your foot on it, you've already traversed it in its entirety. Just to be on this path is to complete it. I mean this literally, not symbolically or metaphorically.

But first you have to step on the path.

This is *right view:* you must have at least a glimmer that there's something difficult, askew, painful, or troubling about human existence.

If it's true that there's something about human life that's off, what would it take to make it "on," so to speak? What would make human existence meaningful or correct? In other words, what do we, as intelligent beings in a vast and apparently meaningless universe, really want? What would answer the hollow ache of the heart? Money? Fame? Sex? Learning? Power? Life in the fast lane? Life in the slow lane? Luxury apartments in Paris and Manhattan? A quiet cottage by a running brook?

Perhaps you can sense already that none of these specifics will do the trick. Indeed, whatever object we pick can at best only temporarily still some particular yearning. The underlying ache of the heart remains omnipresent and unquenchable.

What do you suppose could possibly quench an unquenchable thirst? If it's not an ordinary thirst, then why seek an ordinary cure? It's no use looking for something to take in, to fulfill ourselves. We know that won't work. If we satisfy one craving, another arises to take its place.

What we're dealing with here is a qualitatively different type of problem. So let's take a different approach. For once, let's not attempt to first identify whatever it is we all need and want.

In algebra, we typically label an unknown quantity with a letter such as a, b, or y. We can use the same approach to label what we truly need and want. We'll call it x. X is The Answer. It's what we all really want and need, even though we don't know what it is.

What we do know is that everything we can think of never satisfies us. Thus we know we're looking for something that's not like anything we can think of, or hold as a possession—even as a possession of our minds. Maybe, for a moment now and then, we think or believe there's something that will truly satisfy us. But in the next moment, we discover we're wanting again. Sooner or later, doubts settle back in. By definition, x cannot be like this. If you realized x—whatever it might turn out to be—you'd never want again.

But, unlike the bright objects we commonly pursue in an effort to satisfy ourselves, we cannot seek what we truly need and want because we have no idea what we're searching for. Rather, x is like a fish that swims into the net of its own accord. What we can do—all we can do—is lower the net.

What you really need and want will never appear as an object to your mind. Nevertheless, you already *know* Truth and Reality (what you truly need and want) now. If only you would stop telling yourself what it is, or asking yourself what it might be, or speculating on what it might look like, it would become readily apparent.

Our problem is that we don't pay attention to what we actually *know*. We give our attention to what we think—to what we have ideas or beliefs about—and we discard what we actually *see*.

Starting in ignorance, as we must, we haven't a clue as to what it is that we're going after. Thus we embark on the long search. We may look for Truth in a book, or a creed, or a ritual, or some sacred object or place. But such things never satisfy.

We've got to *see* this and take it to heart. The only thing that truly satisfies is *seeing* Reality—*seeing* what's really going on—in ourselves, others, and the world.

Right view, the first step on the buddha-dharma path, begins not so much in seeing as in realizing the nature of what we're looking for. We stop looking for something that forms as an object in our mind, something we can visualize "out there" and then go after, as if Truth were an image, an idea, or a belief.

Truth is not like this. It's not something to believe or disbelieve. The things we can believe in are always less than Truth and thus cannot satisfy.

Normally, a view of the world is nothing more than a set of beliefs, a way to freeze the world in our minds. But this can never match Reality, simply because the world isn't frozen. Nevertheless we carry on as though the way we've frozen it in our minds is the way it actually is.

When the Buddha spoke of *right view*, he was referring to a view that isn't frozen. *Right view* is fluid and flexible, constantly in motion. It's an awareness of how this moment has come to be.

Right view is *seeing* reality in all its fullness and fluidity. Yet there's nothing in particular to be *seen*.

In the world of our common ordinary mind, everything is divided up: left and right, good and bad, above and below.

For example, we see the puma stalking the deer and we want to call out to the deer to help him escape. And when the puma pounces on the deer, our heart goes out to the deer.

So we look for a way to protect the deer. We put bells on the puma so the deer knows when she's around. As a result, the puma suffers. Eventually, she starves.

With no more puma to keep the deer population in check, the number of deer increases. Before long there are more deer than the local environment can support. The deer overgraze the land and strip the trees and shrubs bare of leaves. And eventually, due to overpopulation, the deer, too, begin to starve.

We believe we're expressing compassion. But compassion must be balanced with wisdom. To the extent we don't *see*, we waste our compassion.

If you *see* Reality in its fluidity and fullness, then you *see* the puma as well as the deer. You *see* how the two fit together as parts of a seamless Whole.

A friend of mine, a physician, told me of his days in medical school when he was overwhelmed with information. He said some teachers could package the information very simply. "Here. This is what you need to know." Medical students loved those teachers, he said.

But there were other teachers who always offered two or more (often contradictory) perspectives on things. This the students hated. "It involved more work on our part," my friend said. "Who wants to be told that some people think this, and some people think that? It was so much easier just to be told what is what."

But, he said, as the years went by and he became more and more experienced as a doctor, he realized that the compact, nicely-packaged views were wrong. The teachers had chopped off all the rough edges that didn't fit into the system.

Sadly, all of us do the same thing, over and over, in virtually every aspect of our lives.

We see this repeatedly in the news. We get the neat little packaged reports—even on complex issues. We're told who the bad guys are, who the good guys are, who the victims are, who the perpetrators are.

What's the driving force that makes us package everything? What we want, what we need, is not to be confused. We want to understand. We want to *know*. Neatly packaging everything gives us the illusion that we actually *know* something. So why do we settle for the simplicity of TV sound bites? Because then we don't have to work so hard. Because we're frightened of grappling with Truth and Reality.

We'd prefer everything nice and neat—this is this, and that is that—everything clearly labeled and laid out. Once we get the world arranged, we'll feel more comfortable—until, like my friend, we look again and say, "Wait a minute! Something's horribly confused. The world makes no sense at all!"

Thus we unwittingly give rise to duhkha.

We have to become comfortable with not knowing—as we commonly think of knowing. Look at the figure below.

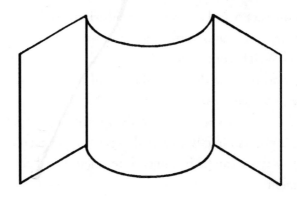

Is it concave or convex?

If we say it's concave, we've taken a view. And because we've taken a view, we've left something out—the fact that the figure could just as easily be considered convex.

And if we say the figure is convex, we've made the exact same mistake. We've merely taken the opposite, equally incomplete position.

Likewise, we may say it's both—but, of course, it's equally neither. (After all, it's not really concave or convex at all, but merely a two-dimensional drawing.)

This is how we commonly deal with the world. By our very attempt to grasp an explanation, we leave things out. In just such a manner, to take any frozen view is to leave out a piece of Reality. What we repeatedly fail to notice is that there is never a static object to observe—nor, for that matter, a static, clearly-defined observer.

What actually goes on is complete fluidity. If we could truly see this, we would cease our insistence on putting boxes, definitions, and beliefs around things. We would have a flexibility of mind that doesn't get bogged down in contradictions. We'd be free from dogmatism, intolerance, arrogance, and insistence on particular outcomes. We'd become comfortable with the fluidity of all things. Indeed, we'd become that very fluidity of mind. We'd have the capacity to tolerate inconceivability.

Right view omits nothing, holds up nothing in particular. Instead, it points directly to actual experience in each moment. The only way we can be free in each moment is to become what the moment is.

Usually we hold a frozen view of ourselves as well as of the world "out there." We think we actually are something. We label ourselves: "I'm a nervous type," "I'm shy and withdrawn," "I always talk with my hands, it's just the way I am." In short, we identify with groups, behaviors, habits, and beliefs.

Because of a strong family identity, I grew up thinking of myself as Norwegian. I was probably in high school before I realized, "Wait a minute! I'm not Norwegian! I was born and raised in Minnesota. I can't speak Norwegian. I've never set foot in Norway. How can I be Norwegian?"

Nowadays, when people learn that I'm an ordained Buddhist priest, they often have some idea about who I must be—even when they have scant knowledge of Buddhism. For example, people often assume I'm a strict vegetarian. And while I never cook and eat meat at home, I have no problem if I'm served meat as a guest. (The Buddha would eat meat if it was served to him. He only refused meat if an animal was slaughtered specifically for him.)

Sometimes people tell me "I'm a Buddhist, too," and wait for me to rejoice in that. But, actually, after thirty years of studying the Buddha's teaching, after priest ordination, after monastic and other kinds of training, I don't think of myself as a Buddhist. Though I am a student and teacher of the buddha-dharma, I don't identify myself with it. Once in a while some event occurs where I'm compelled to step forward as a priest—or as a man, or a Buddhist, or a son, or a friend. But most of the time it's not necessary to wear any hat at all.

When we latch on to an identity, it's easy to take offense. But we offend ourselves. We lock ourselves into very rigid ways of seeing and thinking and feeling and reacting.

It doesn't have to be this way. The fact is, I'm not anything in particular. Nor are you. Nor is anyone.

Another kind of bondage we place ourselves in is the concept "*A* means *B*." It's a concise way of packaging the world. But is it ever possible for "this" to truly mean "that"?

This freezing and framing of the world in conceptual packages provides us with innumerable explanations, none of which can adequately substitute for Reality itself—and none of which can quiet the ache of the heart.

The fact is, Reality doesn't need to be explained. Indeed, it's the one thing that doesn't need explaining. Truth and Reality are self-evident. What's to explain regarding *thus*—regarding the world as it actually is? What can we say about *thus* that doesn't remove us from it? The moment we try to capture and encapsulate Truth, we have paradox, confusion, contention, doubt, and strife.

We make this mistake repeatedly—and we only rarely notice we're making it. Instead, we search for an ever more detailed, complex, and "accurate" form of encapsulation. But what purpose does it serve to deny actual experience in order to run with an idea instead?

We can't comprehend Reality with our intellects. We can't pull it into a static view of some thing. All our explanations are necessarily provisional. They're just rigid frames of what is actually motion and fluidity. In other words, if you can think of how Reality is, you can be sure that's how it isn't. Reality simply cannot be put into a conceptual form—not even through analogy, for there's nothing like it. Reality simply doesn't fit into concepts at all.

Nevertheless, Reality is something you can *see.* You can't conceive of it, but you can perceive it.

For example, if I pointed to a picture of you at the age of two and asked, "Is that you?" what would you say? If you look carefully, you'll *see* that you can't get a conceptual handle on what I'm asking without getting thoroughly entangled in contradictions. I've put this question to hundreds of students in my classes over the years, and I've found the response to be almost predictable. Most people will say without hesitation, "Yes, that's me."

When I point out that they are not babies, the class usually falls silent. After a pause, a lone voice will invariably call out, "That *was* me."

But how can you change (become other than what you are) and still be you? What do we suppose the word "I" refers to? Try as we will, we'll not find any workable, definable thing in actual experience for this "I" to refer to.

The simple fact is, the moment we put anything into a conceptual package, we get a contradiction. Nevertheless, we can always *see* what's going on. As long as we don't ask the question, it's all perfectly clear: what exists in this moment is the picture of a baby, and a grown person pondering how *that* could be *this*.

We habitually fail to notice that by clinging to a concept—in this case, "I"—immediate Reality escapes our grasp. Whenever we conceptualize, we create contradictions that we can't escape. But it's not that Reality is contradictory; it's just that it won't fit into a conceptual frame.

Ideas, of course, aren't the only type of conceptual objects. A concept is anything with a skin around it, some sort of boundary dividing something from something else. Even what we think of as physical objects are actually concepts. For example, you're looking at what is called a book. You can think of it as a book because you conceive of it as separate from other things. In fact, however, it's intimately connected with everything else in the universe.

Thich Nhat Hanh, the prominent Vietnamese Zen master, would remind us that this book is not merely this book, it is the sun as well. After all, if not for the sun, trees would not grow to produce the pulp to make paper. And we cannot forget Ts'ai Lun, who invented paper in the second century, or Johann Gutenberg, who found a way to apply movable type to a printing press in the fifteenth century, or the teams of people who invented and programmed my computer, or the people who taught their teachers.

And intermixed with the trees and the sun and creative human minds are other things. We cannot ignore language, time, soil, plants, animals, emotions, or thoughts. We cannot forget the rain, or even the stars, or the galaxies of stars. Indeed, there is nothing we can point to, or even imagine, that does not find its way into this book either by thought or material.

So, what is what we call "book"?

In a famous Zen story, Emperor Wu of China asked the Buddhist teacher Bodhidharma, "Who are you?"

Bodhidharma replied, "Not knowing."

There's no identity there. Bodhidharma *sees* Reality, not a thing with a name. In other words, *right view* isn't in the eyes of the beholder. There is no beholder of *right view*.

Right intention, the second aspect of the eightfold path, is what most distinguishes a buddha from those of us who are not awake. Why? Because in the moment we are awake, for all practical purposes we're without intention. We could say that the intention of an awakened person is just simply to be awake.

If we want to break the chain of suffering and confusion, our intention should only be to awaken. If our intention is partly to get something from being awake, however, this is already delusion. We don't get anything from being awake. If you're awake, you're just awake. And if you're awake, you'll act and speak in a way that doesn't do injury to yourself or to others.

Of course, in the very next moment we must awaken again. We have to keep coming back to *this* moment.

Thus *right intention* is simply the intention to come back to this moment—to just be present with no ideas of gaining whatsoever. You cannot be *here* and hold a gaining idea at the same time. Just becoming *here* and *now* is enough.

There's a Zen story of the fellow who sat in meditation in order to become a buddha—not an unfamiliar intention among Zen students. His teacher came by and asked, "What are you doing?"

The student replied, "I'm meditating to become a buddha."

The teacher picked up a tile and started to polish it.

"What are you doing?" asked the student.

"I intend to polish this tile into a mirror."

"No amount of polishing will make that tile into a mirror."

"No amount of meditating will make you into a buddha."

We can't approach meditation as if it's a means to something. In fact, we can say that meditation is nothing other than the intention to wake up.

It's important that we have a scheduled time for meditation, but we shouldn't think we're in meditation merely because we've come to a particular place where meditation is practiced and waited for the starting bell to ring. It's not as if now we're meditating, and when the bell rings again, we're done. Meditation isn't like that. It neither begins nor ends. At least not with a bell.

Meditation begins and ends with your intention. If you lose track of your intention to be awake, you're no longer in meditation. If you intend to meditate, then you must do your meditation *now*. Meditation is simply to be here, *now*. If you want to meditate, meditate now—even as you read this book.

If your intention is only to be awake, but you don't know what being awake is, what are you going to do? You can't create some idea about enlightenment and then set out to get it. Awakening isn't like that. If you want to be awake, you must awaken *now*. Come to *this* moment. Be aware of what is going on. Be aware of your intention, right *now*. If you would be in *this* moment, then be awake in *this* moment. That's all. It's very simple.

If you have ideas about this—what it is, what you're going to get from it—it's already delusion. Conception. Ordinary, everyday stuff. Business as usual. *Right intention* is almost like no intention at all. You don't intend to use *right intention* for something else. In fact, it's impossible to do so. The only reason to be awake is to be awake.

If we're not expecting to get anything from being awake, what reason do we have to awaken? There isn't any reason. You already know what not being awake is. It's confusion. It's pain. It's suffering. It's duhkha. If you're getting tired of that, why don't you stop?

"But isn't that wanting to get something?" we ask.

Well, if we approach it in that way, then we haven't stopped it, have we? We're like the fellow in the old joke who goes to the doctor. He reaches behind his back with his right hand to touch his left elbow and says, "Doc, it hurts when I do this." The doctor looks at him and replies, "Then don't do that."

We're never called on to do what hurts. We just do what hurts out of ignorance and habit. Once we *see* what we're doing, we can stop.

Right intention simply means that your mind isn't leaning. Your ordinary mind assumes there's something "out there." Either you want it and you try to get it, or you dislike it and try to keep it away. To the extent your mind leans either toward or away from certain things, longing and loathing are present. This leaning reveals your state of mind.

The mind doesn't only lean toward the obvious—fame, money, sex, and such—it can lean toward anything. It can even lean toward putting an end to leaning. "Oh yeah, I want enlightenment!" But, of course, this is to lean once again.

The thing you really want is for your mind not to lean. So what are you going to do about it? You may say, "Okay, I'm going to straighten up my mind!" And then you struggle to straighten up your mind.

But that is leaning!

The mind will not be ruled. If you try to get it to lean less, it just leans all the more. So how are we ever going to get our minds to stop leaning? Just attend to what you're doing. Because in attending to this moment, you're attending to your own mind. You're watching your mind lean. *See* how this leaning comes about. When you acquaint yourself with what leaning really is, you'll realize that in trying to stop it from leaning, you're making it lean all the more. Nevertheless, as you watch what actually takes place in each moment, already your mind has begun to lean less.

You cannot make your mind not lean—at least, not directly. But when you observe what actually takes place from moment to moment, the mind, of its own accord, straightens up.

7

Morality

Samuel Johnson said we more often need to be reminded than instructed. The Buddha's words on the practice of *right speech*—the third aspect of the eightfold path—serve as a reminder of what we all already know.

> They speak the truth, are devoted to the truth, reliable, worthy of confidence. . . . They never knowingly deceive others for the sake of their own advantage. . . . What they have heard here, they do not repeat there, so as to cause dissension there. . . . Thus they unite those that are divided, and those that are united they encourage. Concord gladdens them, they delight and rejoice in concord; and it is concord that they spread by their words. They avoid harsh language and speak such words as are gentle, soothing to the ear, loving, going to the heart, cour-

teous and dear, and agreeable to many. They avoid vain talk and speak at the right time, in accordance with facts, speak what is useful, speak about *right wisdom* and *right practice*; their speech is like a treasure, at the right moment accompanied by arguments, moderate and full of sense.

Actually, much of the buddha-dharma is like this. It strikes with strong familiarity. Nevertheless, most of us need to be reminded of what we already *know*.

What's the point of *right speech*? It's to remind ourselves, to constantly bring ourselves back to this moment—not only for ourselves, but for others as well. It's to do whatever leads us out of confusion and bondage. It's to *see* what's really going on.

The Buddha did not lay down any commandments. If we say, "Thou shalt not lie," applying it as a rule, what are we to do when the Gestapo pounds at our door and we're harboring a family of innocent fugitives in the attic? If not lying were an absolute rule to live by, we'd be in deep moral trouble.

Nevertheless, it's not the case that buddhas simply live out of their own individual truths. The buddha-dharma is not about the Buddha's truth, or your truth, or my truth, or another person's truth. The buddha-dharma—what the awakened teach—is about directly *seeing* Truth itself, prior to forming any ideas about it. It is about responding to each particular situation as it comes to be, not according to some lockstep program of do's and don'ts. We can't use a hard and fast rule to deal with the dilemmas and uncertainties and ambiguities of life. A rule—any rule—would only open the door for relativism and contradiction.

Nevertheless, we can *see* what's morally appropriate in each situation. We can easily *see* what actions and speech will lead us and others into hatred, confusion, difficulty, and suffering. And we can *see* what words and actions will not. It all has to do with our intention. Is our intention to hoodwink, mislead, inflate, or deceive others—or is it to be awake?

Here is the focus for *right speech*. In any given moment, our eyes must be open to *see* our situation fully for what it is. Our intent—and the action, speech, and thought that arise from that intent—is that we all become free of our confusion. For this, it's not necessary that we see one thing pitted against another.

Right speech omits nothing. It includes the whole picture: the Gestapo, the fugitive family, yourself, and the world in which you live.

Right speech doesn't rely on judgment or discriminative thinking. In judging we weigh everything out. We base our speech on some conceptual frame that we've arranged to accommodate ourselves and process ideas—like, for example, the idea that the Gestapo are inherently bad, and the people upstairs are inherently good. This is precisely the thinking that got us into trouble in the first place. Indeed, it's the very thinking that produces both the Gestapo and the fugitives.

Instead, we have to simply *see* the situation in all its pain, conflict, difficulty, and contradiction, and *see* how it is we become so confused. Then, and only then, can we speak and act in a way that's conducive to awakening.

We must also observe our own intent, so that we can *know* when we're speaking or acting out of a leaning mind, out of a desire to bring about some particular end. *Right speech* concerns your intention. Are you using speech because you're trying to manipulate the world and other people? Or are you speaking in order to help yourself and others wake up?

When you become a listener, the concern remains the same: to be awake. But how do you do this as a listener? Let's consider this statement from the Buddha about *right speech* again:

> What they have heard here, they do not repeat there, so as to cause dissension there. . . . Thus they unite those that are divided, and those that are united they encourage. Concord gladdens them, they delight and rejoice in concord; and it is concord that they spread by their words.

Now imagine you are the listener. Pat tells you something about Jolene. What do you *just hear* as a listener? What are you actually aware of, as opposed to what you think or believe or decide? What information have you actually received?

You've received information about Pat—not about Jolene.

We tend not to notice this, however. We may walk away believing we have solid information about Jolene. But we don't. All we have are Pat's words about her.

On the other hand, we've received very direct information about Pat, because we've heard his words and intonations, we've seen his gestures, posture, and expressions.

We have to pay attention to our actual circumstance—the situation we're actually in. And what we've actually been presented with is Pat.

A buddha recognizes that anything put into speech is never completely reliable. Whatever someone says to you about another person is skewed from the start. It comes through their filter, their likes and dislikes, their education, their ambition, and the leanings of their own mind.

Perhaps you haven't even met Jolene. If you're wise, you'll withhold judgments about her because, at best, all you really know about Jolene is what Pat thinks of her. If you're not wise, however, you'll accept Pat's words as reality and adopt his view, and his leanings of mind, as your own. Then, when you finally do meet Jolene, you'll bring to the encounter a prejudiced view—one that isn't even your own.

Fritz Pfeffer, the dentist who hid from the Nazis along with Anne Frank and her family, is seen in a negative light by masses of people, simply because all most of us have ever heard of him comes from the words of a young, inexperienced—although brilliant and imaginative—person, Anne Frank. We get another picture from Miep Gies, who harbored the Franks and saved Anne's diary. She called Pfeffer a "lovely, lovely man."

In Kurosawa's movie *Rashomon*, we're told different versions of the same story by different characters. First we see the event through the eyes of a woodcutter, and we think we know what happened. But as the story unfolds we meet up with each of the remaining characters, and each tells his or her version of what happened. And each character tells a different story. One of the things that comes across in this movie is how easily we're swayed by the first story we hear.

This is the situation we face in life. As little children, we readily accept the first story we're given at home, or school, or church. We're told stories of nationalism, religion, racism, politics, and family. All too often we accept them before we learn to weigh them against other views. And all too often we're inclined to accept these (or other) frozen views rather than *see* each situation for what it is.

So *right speech* also involves *right listening*—which means observing things as they are, rather than accepting some prepackaged, easy-to-swallow story.

When we talk about others, we should be very careful to observe our motive—especially if we're talking about a person who isn't present. Are we trying to knock the person down and raise ourselves up? Or are we trying to raise up or inflate the other person? Either way, we're not speaking in a way that is conducive to awakening, because we're following the leanings of our mind rather than what we *see*.

Furthermore, when we speak about people based on what we think, feel, or hope rather than on what we observe and experience, we deprive them of their humanity. We have replaced what they are, in all their fluid vitality, with our own crystallized ideas, opinions, and beliefs.

In short, when we don't attend to what we *see* or *know*, but run with what we imagine, we create problems.

In many ways, we create a bigger problem when we put people on a pedestal in our speech than when we cut them down. Whenever we make anyone—a minister, a teacher, an athlete, a genius, our ancestors, the Buddha—bigger than life, it's easy for both you and your listener to forget that the person you're discussing is a human being. And with the passing of time, the person will only become larger until, like Paul Bunyan, they're sixty ax-handles high.

We tend to bunyanize the people we admire. But this is very dangerous—particularly if your hero is a teacher of the buddha-dharma. You'll forget that you're made of the very same stuff they are. You'll forget that, like them, you're completely equipped to *see* Truth right here, right now.

If you keep putting an enlightened person (or, more accurately, your concept of "an enlightened person") on a pedestal, you'll miss this critical point, and get lost in confusion. As long as you think enlightenment is something special, you won't wake up.

One of the things my own Zen teacher taught me was (as he put it): "Final job of teacher: free student of teacher."

How, then, are you going to allow teachers to finish their work if you keep bunyanizing them? You'll turn your teachers into something grandiose and vain. If you would honor a teacher, you would only need to learn from that teacher, respectfully test their teachings against your own experience, and live with a grateful heart.

I remember hearing a fellow talking about the Nazi doctors on the radio. He described these people as monsters, subhuman. It's true, of course, that we human beings have done monstrous things. But none of us is anything other than human. Indeed, it's because we're human that we are capable of such monstrous actions. If we don't realize this—that every sadistic murderer is human, like us—then we overlook the fact that we have the capacity to act as they do.

We have to realize what we are. The range of what is human is vast, ranging from the saintly to the monstrous. When we speak of other human beings as if they somehow do not belong to our species, we ignore the reality of our very nature.

My Zen teacher used to say, "Kind speech is not always kind." Generally, of course, a gentle word or compliment is most conducive to serenity, goodwill, and waking up. But, just as you would not refuse to vaccinate your child because the procedure is painful, once in a while there's that fleeting moment where the kindest thing you can do for another is to utter a severe word or sharp observation that may hurt momentarily. The child who's about to dash into a busy street may need to be told sharply to stop.

Before you speak, you must examine your own mind and motive. If you're trying to put someone down, or if you're about to speak from malice or spite, then don't speak at all. But if in that moment you must tell someone, "I'm saddened by how you treated Jim this morning. I think you owe him an apology," then say it. Or perhaps for a friend's health, sanity, and well-being, you need to say, "I think you've got a problem with alcohol. If you continue to drink as you do now, you will accomplish little else. And you will cause your family to suffer as well." It could hurt. It could appear very cutting at that moment, from the outside. But that doesn't necessarily mean it's not kind. It depends on your motive. Be sure to first observe your own mind. It's impossible to specify a proper response in advance. Every situation must be dealt with on a case-by-case basis.

If you would awaken, the point is not so much to be concerned with the actual words you speak, or even their tone. Instead, be concerned with observing your own heart and mind. Then speak out of your awareness of what you observe—in your heart, mind, and situation. The words you select, and their tone, will follow appropriately. And you will be speaking and listening out of wisdom and compassion.

If you try to speak of Truth or Reality, you can't say what it is, because it won't fit into words or concepts. This is why we get so frustrated with enlightenment. We can't put our finger on it. We can't get it into our hands.

We're used to getting a conceptual handle on things. (And when we don't, we often abandon them.) But Truth doesn't go into concepts. We can't hold it as an idea. We literally can't speak Truth.

When we *see* Reality, we are completely beyond the realm of words and concepts. We experience what words cannot express, what ideas cannot contain, what speech cannot communicate.

So, in a sense, there's nothing to say.

Picture a maple tree in late fall. Most of the leaves have fallen. Only a few leaves remain attached to the tree.

You're sitting in a park. It's a beautiful day—warm for this time of year. The sky is a brilliant deep blue. Against the sky, near the top of a tree, you see a single leaf. It's a very bright reddish-orange. As you're looking at it the leaf quivers and begins to fall. It tumbles down, drifting across the sky. You turn your head slightly to follow it. It drifts down, slowly, then lands on the ground in a place where many other leaves have fallen before.

You look at the pattern of leaves on the ground. You notice how, near the tree, there are more leaves and how, further from the tree, there are fewer. As your eyes pass over the grass toward the next tree, you find more leaves on the ground once again.

You raise your gaze a bit and look out across the lawn. You see places where there are more leaves, and places where there are fewer leaves. Wherever you look, however, there are always beautiful patterns of varying color.

Who or what can make such patterns?

Ryokan, a Japanese Zen poet of the late eighteenth and early nineteenth centuries, wrote this simple poem:

> *Maple leaf*
> *Falling down*
> *Showing front*
> *Showing back*

The action of a maple leaf falling down, showing front, showing back—the way it falls from the tree, when it falls from the tree, how it falls from the tree, where it lands—all of this exemplifies *right action*. How different this kind of action is from the kinds of willed, goal-oriented action we're so familiar with!

Imagine a maple leaf that says in midsummer, "I'm checkin' out. I'm gettin' off this tree." And there it goes, tumbling down while still green. Or imagine the leaf that just won't let go. It hangs on all winter, not willing to move or change, until next year's bud gives it the boot. Then there's the leaf that doesn't want to be "just a leaf in the wind." When it falls from the branch, it curls up and does a cannonball to the ground.

What kind of pattern would these leaves make on the ground? It would be quite different from the one described by Ryokan.

Leaves, of course, have no motives. We human beings, however, operate in all three of these ways on quite a regular basis. In attempting to exert control over people, things, and events, we run away, hang on tightly, or thumb our noses and do what we please.

The action of Ryokan's slowly drifting maple leaf—natural, unwilled—demonstrates *right action*. The actions of the other leaves, which I've illustrated in a silly way, are willed. These two types of actions lead to quite different results.

Usually, discussions of morality never stray too far from rules and regulations, from thou-shalts and thou-shalt-nots. Remember the Buddhist precepts from Chapter Five? Even these are often taught and learned as rules. But rules and regulations are not what the buddha-dharma is about. Rules and regulations are only handy when we don't *see*. The point of precepts is to *see*, to live in accordance with Reality, not to follow rules blindly. If you *see*, you don't need rules. In fact, rules become a hindrance. They bind our natural freedom of mind. In *seeing*, your actions become like leaves that land in the natural spot on the lawn.

In *Zen Mind, Beginner's Mind*, Zen Master Shunryu Suzuki pointed out that if we try to put dots on paper in "artistic disorder," such disorder will not come as easily as we might think. As you put one dot after another on the page, you want them to go onto the page as leaves land on a lawn. But it quickly becomes difficult to build up a truly random pattern. Why? It has to do with the difference between *right action* and rules, precepts, and commandments.

We tend to set our minds in rigid forms of will. We unwittingly follow hidden assumed rules which manifest in habitual patterns of thought and behavior. Such actions aren't born out of *seeing* the Whole. And that *seeing*, that unfettered thought and movement, is what we would need to arrange dots in a truly random pattern.

Instead, we tend to be more like the leaf that decides to curl up and cannonball out of the tree. We'd rather sing, "I'll do it my way," believing this to be an expression of freedom.

We have it entirely backward.

We might counter with, "What should I be? Just a leaf in the wind? That's not so good!" But the fact of the matter is, that is just what you are. Indeed, you are indistinguishable from the wind itself.

Yet we resist. We don't allow ourselves to land in the natural spot, or to become the natural pattern. Instead, we try to control the situation. The results of these attempts is duhkha—longing, wanting, craving, and the pain of confusion.

When we fancy ourselves to be a particular thing with a name, we see ourselves as we would a cork in a stream. What we do not realize is that there is only stream. What we fancy as particular is, from the first, only movement, change and flow.

The recognition of this as our actual experience is utter release from duhkha.

Seeing alone carries us to greater levels of moral development. Through *seeing*, by and by, we need not live merely by rules. Indeed, to completely mature morally as human beings, we must learn to operate in a place where rules will often be insufficient.

The saint simply lives by *seeing*. Some Buddhists call such a person a bodhisattva. When we meet such a person, we're sometimes awestruck. We see what they do, and then we start to write down rules that seem to describe it. It looks like we ought to not lie, not steal, not kill, and so forth.

Yes, the saintly person doesn't lie, we've noticed. But why don't they? Is it because they think it's against the rules? Because they think it's evil? Because they fear punishment? Because they don't want to look bad in the eyes of others? Not really. Rather, they avoid lying, stealing, and killing because they *see* the natural repercussions of such behavior. They *see* that it leads to confusion, to suffering—to duhkha. They don't do it because they *see* the Whole scene.

We generally come to the question of *right action* as we come to almost everything . . . we want to have the right answer, something we can encapsulate in a handy slogan. But try as we might, though it can be *seen*, morality defies any attempt we make to harness it.

For example, let's consider what is widely thought of as the finest of all moral laws, the golden rule: "Do unto others as you would have them do unto you." This rule appears in virtually all societies. If there were a universal rule to live by, surely this one is it. In fact, however, it's deeply flawed. We can *see* this without much difficulty. Indeed, you may have *seen* it for yourself already.

Suppose I'm a rough, cantankerous fellow who enjoys nothing better than getting into fist fights. I always obey the golden rule, because I only do to others what I would have done unto me. So, wherever I go, I always get into fights.

Clearly, there's a problem here. It's because of this flaw that moral philosophers have tried to rephrase the golden rule to make it work in all cases. One popular reformulation has been what is called the inversion of the golden rule. This says: "Do unto other as they would have you do unto them."

But this is still problematic. If the person you're dealing with is a child who sits at the dinner table screaming "I don't want to eat my peas, I want to eat candy," you'd be obliged to feed the child candy instead of a nourishing meal. Obviously, your moral obligation to the child can't be dictated merely by what the child demands or wants. There needs to be something more basic than this. But what?

It seems we cannot live satisfactorily without morality, yet it seems equally true that we have no clear basis whatsoever for morality. As W. Macneile Dixon put it:

> Probably upon no subject ever discussed through the length and breadth of the globe has there been expended a fiercer hubbub of words than upon this—the foundations of morality. "Why should I ask God to make me good when I want to be naughty?" asked the little girl. All the wise men of the world are put to silence by this childish query. A parliament of philosophers will not resolve it. When we set out in search of an answer we are . . . lost.

It's not a rule that's required, but *seeing*. The bodhisattva lives by *seeing*, not by rule. What's required is to *see* the Whole. Through *seeing*, it's possible to reformulate the golden rule without creating problems like those described above. Of course, in this reformulation, it's no longer a rule—a frozen directive—at all.

It so happens, however, that the way the awakened would put it is one of the formulations Western philosophy has rejected: "Do not do unto others what you would not have done unto you."

The reason this formulation has been generally overlooked in Western philosophy is because the positive formulation is thought to be more . . . well, positive. While the positive formulation would have us get out there and do something, the negative formulation seems passive.

Yet this habitual response overlooks the fact that the positive formulation always presents us with intractable problems, problems that simply don't occur with the negative formulation at all. Why? What's the difference? It has to do with will, motive, and intention. These are all deeply entangled in the positive formulation. The positive formulation tells you what you should do. The negative formulation is not prescriptive.

This is the crux of the problem. There can be no final moral authority to tell you what to do, for no such authority can lie outside your own will. In other words, in order for you to be a moral agent, you must have the final authority. And indeed you do. It's precisely because we have such authority that we must take our willed actions into account. It's willed action that binds us to duhkha, to pain and confusion.

The negative formulation of the golden rule is not a rule, exactly, but more a precept. It doesn't entangle us in unresolvable quandaries because it doesn't draw upon volition. With the negative formulation, only our one-pointed intention to be awake is called upon. Actions are initiated by *seeing*, not by formula.

The simple fact is that we cannot have a rule stating what we should do, or how we should do it. The moment we positively assert such a thing we have precisely what we would not have— a narrow, brittle, prepackaged, inflexible morality. And once again we've opened a door that lets us abandon immediate Reality in favor of our beliefs and ideas *about* Reality. Without reference to any rule, like the bodhisattva, we already *see* the cause of sorrow. As for what we should do, this only becomes apparent by *seeing*. It's always case-by-case. There isn't any rule for it.

Here's the basis for *right action*: to refrain from all that is divisive and contentious, to do what promotes harmony and unity. In short, it's to act out of *seeing* the Whole. It's to live as a falling leaf—as the streaming wind itself.

This is not a prescribed state of mind. It's not a state of mind that says, "I've got to do good." This approach simply does not work.

We tend to think of good as something opposed to evil. But this is just our idea of good. It's "good" crystallized. It breeds arrogance and hostility. To act in a way that is truly good is radically different from our ordinary way. It is to act with a mind that is neither programmed, hindered, nor perturbed. It is to act in a way that speaks of the Whole. Like a falling leaf.

Another way to understand *right action* is to think of it as selfless action, action done while free of a sense of self. Action in which you don't see yourself as separate from other things.

This is not to say that consciousness itself has winked out and nothing is happening. Perception is still there, of course. There's still physical sensation, including pain and pleasure. It's just that "you" are not there. And with the sense of self gone, "your" actions naturally become uncalculated and free.

This occurs when your will has been filed down to a single point. Your only intention is to be awake, be present. Your actions are appropriate and free, like a leaf falling naturally from the tree.

This is total freedom of mind.

When we insist on hanging onto our branch, in our ignorance we think this is freedom. "I can do what I want, and if I feel like falling in midsummer, I will. And if I want to cannonball, it's my business." We don't *see* that what we're calling freedom is actually bondage.

When we act this way, we become prisoners of our own whims and desires. As a result, we're unable to act out of *seeing* our situation for what it is, moment after moment. We're only able to act according to our cravings.

We think that freedom lies in making choices based on our desires. But when we *see* our circumstances, we see much more than just our desires. We see how the current situation has come to be.

True freedom doesn't lie in having choices. We always have no choice but to act. Even if we choose not to act, we're still acting—and still making a choice.

Our only choice of consequence lies in whether or not we're awake.

Right livelihood, the fifth aspect of the eightfold path, involves earning your living in a manner that doesn't bring harm to yourself or others.

There are a few ways to earn a living that can be clearly identified as not conducive to awakening—trafficking in drugs or weapons or slavery, writing propaganda for repressive governments, and so forth. And there are many ways of earning a living that don't seem clearly moral or clearly immoral at all.

Just what is *right livelihood* when we live in such a tangled social and economic web? It's difficult to find any means of livelihood that does absolutely no harm to anyone, since everything we might do is so deeply enmeshed with everything else.

What about a profession like law? Surely as a lawyer you might often have the chance to do something beneficial, such as defending an innocent human being or challenging an unreasonable and repressive law. But you might also be asked to defend someone you know perfectly well is guilty, or to lobby for an organization or industry that is utterly unconcerned with people's welfare. You may also have a family to support.

In walking the path of the awakened, we're invited to look at this matter of livelihood very carefully. Indeed, we can't ignore it, because the issue will remain a serious one for most of our lives. There are no clear-cut rules to follow here. You must simply *see* the situation you're in.

If you're in a profession that's clearly caught up in something pernicious and hurtful to people, maybe you should get out. Or maybe you should stay in the field and do what you can to make it more humane. Or perhaps the best course is to look for a similar job in a more compassionate industry, even if that means taking a cut in pay.

You must observe your own particular circumstances carefully, then act. Observe your attitude as you engage in your work. *See* what produces entanglements, desire, suffering. *See* what produces harmony, joy, goodwill, cooperation, and peace of mind. If you have trouble sleeping at night, look at how you earn your living. This is often where the problem resides. You must learn to *see* clearly, and thus do what is most conducive to awakening.

We cannot judge others, but must each examine our own life.

The buddha-dharma is about examining our lives, our behavior, our speech, and the means by which we earn our keep on this planet—and how all these activities connect with everything else.

We have only one choice. Either we awaken, or we do not.

8

Practice

Just sit for a moment and relax. Take a couple of deep breaths. Now: try not to think of an elephant.

Here's something else to contemplate: picture a square circle. Try harder. Make an effort.

As you've probably realized already, both of these exercises are by nature impossible.

Often, though, we put our efforts into tasks very much like these. We focus our energies on goals that are impossible, or where the means to bring about our goals are entirely out of our hands. Thus we often think of effort as a kind of straining, or forcing, or pushing. But with what the Buddha called *right effort*—the sixth aspect of the eightfold path—there's no straining, no forcing, no pushing, partly because *right effort* is conjoined with *right view*. When you actually *see* that putting your hand in a flame is painful, you don't need to strain to keep yourself from doing it.

Right effort means simply being present. It means being here, staying here, and to *see* what's happening in this moment. It's not about trying to control, trying to bring something about—like straining to achieve enlightenment. This is much like trying not to think of an elephant. *Right effort* is naturalness—naturalness of movement, naturalness of thought. It's the naturalness of becoming this moment.

This is not how we usually understand effort. Usually we make an effort to control, or be different, or try something new, or improve the situation, or improve ourselves. Human history is filled with this kind of effort.

And here we are with our improved human world that we've spent a great deal of time and energy working on. We've improved the rivers and the lakes and the land and our society and our ways of living to the point where we now wonder if the human race will survive.

Right effort is, first of all, cutting off the fragmented and fractured states of mind that have already arisen in us. In these common states of mind, the world appears "out there," divided in various ways, with one thing set against another. When we're in such a state of mind, we *see* things as needing to be manipulated and controlled. The Buddha called such a state of mind "unwholesome" because it doesn't take in the whole scene that's being presented to us.

We have to *see* where we can effectively apply our effort and where we can't. When we're not *seeing* we'll put most, if not all, of our energy into the areas where we have no control. We'll try to control situations, people, and things over which, in fact, we have little or no influence. Sometimes we'll try to control our own inclinations and impulses. But it's all a lot like trying not to think of an elephant.

We must first *see* what we can control and what we can't. Otherwise we'll waste our effort in trying to do the impossible while ignoring what is easily within reach.

Most of the time our mental state is fragmented. Our mind is filled with thoughts like "I'm going to get what I can out of this," or "I must do something for those people," or "I wish my mental state weren't so scattered." Or it could be any one of the countless other ways we set one thing off against another.

But what should our effort be? To drive off such thoughts like a herd of elephants? We already know, they'll not be driven off. The more we try to push them away, the more we feed them, and the more they grow in strength and staying power.

If we simply observe our fragmented mental state instead, *seeing* it for what it is rather than feeding it—whether by judging it, indulging in it, or trying to shoo it away—then it collects into full awareness of its own accord.

The effort involved in gathering your scattered mind isn't an effort directly applied to a particular situation through your force of will. It doesn't follow from thinking, "I see my unwholesome state of mind. Now I have to cut it off." That isn't going to work. Simply by *seeing* your state of mind, by *seeing* your inclinations toward this and away from that, you are awake. All you have to do is to continue bringing yourself back to *seeing*. To *see* is to heal an otherwise fragmented mind and to prevent further scattering of mind from occurring.

Right effort is also bringing about and preserving aware, collected, wholesome, and integrated states of mind.

We all know the maxim "You can lead a horse to water, but you can't make him drink." It's because we want the horse to drink that we become frustrated, because it's literally not in our power to accomplish the job we've set out to do for ourselves.

We so often insist on a particular outcome. We expect our objective to be met if we apply ourselves to the task directly, earnestly, and with sufficient energy of will. We want that person to shape up, the government to cut taxes, the environment to be cleaned up, and all wars to stop.

But if you want to wake up, forget outcomes. Instead, observe your own inclination of mind.

When it comes to the buddha-dharma, we're actually the horse who is being led to water. The awakened lead us to water. They point the way. But we have to drink. That job is our own.

Things can be pointed out to us, but unless we take them to heart—examine them carefully, test them respectfully, digest them thoroughly, and make them come alive in our life—we won't wake up. We must make that effort ourselves.

There's more to this metaphor. The horse is actually thirsty. And if this realization is strong enough, the horse is going to drink. But first the horse must recognize that it is water—something easily in reach—that he needs. Otherwise he will waste away, even while he stands at the water trough.

Our ignorance is such that most of us don't realize we're thirsty. Or, if we realize we're thirsty, we look for water in the wrong place. We go into fire looking for cool refreshment. And often we're confused about what our thirst actually is.

Usually, if something seems valuable to us, we feel we have to work hard to get it or move toward it. In the case of awakening, this doesn't work. In fact, it takes us further away from the realm of awakening.

A fellow went to a Zen master and said, "If I work very hard, how soon can I be enlightened?"

The Zen master looked him up and down and said, "Ten years."

The fellow said, "No, listen, I mean if I really work at it, how long—"

The Zen master cut him off. "I'm sorry. I misjudged. Twenty years."

"Wait!" said the young man, "You don't understand! I'm—"

"Thirty years," said the Zen master.

The young man eloquently expresses our usual way. But we're not dealing with usual stuff here. We can't take this approach if our goal is a non-obsessed mind.

Our effort to awaken is like aiming at a reverse target. As with all targets, we want to hit the bull's-eye. But this is the bull's-eye of enlightenment. And if that's what you're aiming at, you can't do it with a leaning mind. You can't want enlightenment like you want other things. There's absolutely nothing to go after. So how do we hit it? How do we wake up?

Normally a target is arranged so that the closer you get to the center, the more points you get. But the target of enlightenment is reversed. The big dot in the center is zero points. The small ring that surrounds it is worth ten points. The one outside that is worth twenty-five. And the hundred-point ring is way out around the outer edge of the target. If you want to score points, you're better off shooting wide. But if you truly want to awaken, you'll have to hit the bull's-eye at dead center.

The closer you come to the pupil of the bull's-eye without hitting dead center, the further away you are from awakening. In other words, if you're only going after robes, chants, rituals, or a Buddhist name, you'll be far more off the mark than if you had never begun to study the buddha-dharma in the first place. These things are cultural accretions that have accumulated over millennia. They have nothing to do with awakening, and will probably distract you from the urgent task at hand.

Unlike archery, hitting the center of the bull's-eye of enlightenment does not require skill, in the usual sense. Just put your effort into being awake in this moment. Simply remember what your business on the path is—waking up—and then return to right here, right now.

Most of the time, most of the people we meet are at best only partially engaged in the moment. And often we find people (or ourselves) lost in thought or reverie—barely here at all.

It was a spring morning. I was on one of my daily walks around a nearby lake. The light was luscious; the flowers were beginning to bloom; the smells were heady. Suddenly I heard the loud squawking of geese.

I looked up to *see* a flock of twenty or more birds, flying in formation almost at eye level, coming right at me. They came in fast, like the edge of a blanket being pulled over my head. As they passed over me, I could hear the rush of air over their wings.

At that same moment, also coming toward me, was a jogger with earphones. Still squawking loudly, the geese passed right over the jogger's head—some canting a bit to avoid hitting her.

What I found more astounding than the geese was the fact that she kept jogging. She didn't notice the geese at all. I wanted to share this remarkable event with her, even if only through a glance or a smile. But she wasn't present.

How often we miss the moment simply because we're not here. We tune out much of the world—and much of ourselves as well—just as that jogger did. And generally we don't even realize how removed we are from what is going on.

The Buddha constantly pointed out the seriousness of this condition. In fact, to the awakened, its consequences are total. "Those who are aware," he said, "do not die. Those who are ignorant are as if dead already." Life is only lived in this moment, which is fleeting, changing constantly. We can't grasp it. If only we'd stop embalming life, freezing it into a view, we'd experience life as it is, and at its fullest. The importance of *right mindfulness*, the seventh aspect of the eightfold path, is that it weaves together all seven other aspects of the path, and brings us back to Reality, here and now.

Mindfulness of the body is awareness of how it moves: the position of the hand, head, or tongue; our posture; our breathing; the touch of grass, or sand, or wood, or stone underfoot; and the taste and smell of this moment.

Thich Nhat Hanh, in one of his walking exercises, asks us to imagine we're astronauts who have crashed on the moon. We're stranded. We look up into the sky and see the beautiful blue Earth, but we can't get back to it because our ship is damaged. All we can do is look at that brilliant blue orb in the cold black sky and long to be home again.

But suppose we managed to fix our craft after all, and landed once again, on Earth. How would we feel as we first set foot upon the Earth? What would we observe and savor? How intensely would we experience the smells and flavors, the gentle rain, or the warm sand underfoot?

This, says Thich Nhat Hanh, is how we should walk on the earth with each step.

Just as we can attend to the body and to our physical surroundings, we can also take note of the present emotional backdrop of our mind. By simply attending to how we feel without trying to judge or change our feelings, we may notice that there's no real distinction to be made between self and other. If it's a gray day inside, then it's a gray day outside as well.

Over time we may also notice that each feeling we experience is transitory and impermanent. Eventually, through simple observation, our feelings, while no less vivid, will become less urgent, and will cease to have such a firm hold on our emotions and actions. We will be able to *see* each feeling as it arises without feeling compelled to act on it.

If, in observing your feelings, an inner commentary begins—"This is good," "This is bad," "I don't like this"—just be aware that such comments are being made. You don't have to make the further comment "I should be watching rather than commenting." Simply attend to your background feeling. Don't try to alter it, just note it for what it is.

There's also mindfulness of mind. Until we deliberately listen for it, we usually pay little attention to the fact that there's the constant chatter of a monologue—often idiotic—running in our minds. When we really lose ourselves, we can even work it up into a dialogue.

Our minds jabber to themselves much of the time. If you don't think so, just sit quietly for a moment and try to remain aware of your breathing, noting when you breathe in and when you breathe out. If you do this even for five minutes you will probably notice that throughout that time your mind has toyed with innumerable thoughts, feelings, and fantasies.

Our unobserved mind is the source of a great deal of confusion and suffering for us. We habitually act out of our thoughts and assumptions—most of which we're only vaguely aware of— rather than out of full engagement with the moment. To make matters worse, we often identify with our thoughts, as if substantiality could somehow be found in what we think or believe. When we carefully observe our minds we cannot help but note that our thoughts and mental states are just as fleeting as the sensations of our bodies.

Finally, there is mindfulness of duhkha itself: how and why it appears, and how to bring about its cessation.

We need to become mindful of the out-of-kilterness in human life. We need to *see* that this out-of-kilterness arises within our own hearts and minds. Finally, we can come to *see* that duhkha can be put to an end by walking the eightfold path.

A key point in the practice of mindfulness is never to chastise yourself. When you realize you haven't been mindful, don't scold yourself. There's no need for it—in fact, it gets in your way. It's only necessary that you notice that you were not mindful although, of course, in doing so, you are being mindful. Just watch your mind. When you learn to *see* what is painful and not conducive to awakening you'll stop doing it, very naturally.

While *right mindfulness* is to return to actual experience, *right meditation*, the eighth aspect of the eightfold path, is simply staying with our immediate experience, moment by moment.

In sitting meditation (*zazen* in Japanese), the focus of our activity involves the bare minimum—just body, mind, and breath. If at all possible, it's best to receive instruction in sitting meditation from an experienced teacher rather than from a book. It's also best to meditate with others. Nevertheless, for formal written instruction, I can do no better than quote Zen Master Dogen from his "Universal Recommendation for Sitting Meditation" (*Fukanzazengi*):

> For meditation, a quiet room is suitable. Eat and drink moderately. Cast aside all involvements and cease all affairs. Do not think good or bad. Do not administer pros and cons. Cease all the movements of the conscious mind, the gauging of all thoughts and views. Have no designs on becoming a buddha. Meditation has nothing whatever to do with sitting or lying down.
>
> At the site of your regular sitting, spread out thick matting and place a cushion above it. Sit in a cross-legged position with your knees directly upon the mat. You should have your clothes and belt loosely bound and arranged in order. Then place your right hand on your left leg and your left palm facing upwards on your right palm, thumb tips touching. Thus sit upright in correct bodily posture, neither inclining to the left nor to the right, neither leaning forward nor backward. Be sure your ears are on a plane with your shoulders and your nose in line with your navel. Place your tongue against the front roof of your mouth, with teeth and lips both shut. Your

eyes should always remain open, and you should breathe gently through your nose.

Once you have adjusted your posture, take a deep breath, inhale and exhale, rock your body right and left and settle into a steady, immobile sitting position.

This instruction is for meditating while sitting on the floor, but you can also meditate sitting in a chair. Place your feet squarely on the floor. Adjust the height of the chair with a pad or blanket if necessary so that you sit with your thighs parallel to the floor. Keep your back straight; do not lean against the back of the chair.

If you choose to sit on a cushion on the floor, adjust the height of the cushion to ensure that your knees rest on the mat. If you prefer a kneeling posture, you may wish to support your body by placing a cushion between your legs.

After you have rocked your body and settled into your sitting position, bring your attention to your breath. Sitting erect, breathe fully and deeply from your diaphragm. Breathe from the center of your body. Place your focus on your breath. Breathe naturally and quietly. Don't force the breath in any way—just follow it. As you inhale, be aware of breathing in. As you exhale, be aware of breathing out.

In the beginning stages, since it's difficult to stay with the breath, counting each breath may help you maintain your concentration. Count one as you inhale, two as you exhale. Continue counting to ten, then repeat.

Again, just follow the breath. As you do, thoughts will arise. Don't be bothered by them. Don't think they're bad, or that you shouldn't be having them. Don't try to drive them away. If you leave them alone, they'll depart of their own accord. This is how to "cease all the movements of the conscious mind." You cannot do it by direct application of your will.

If you find you've been distracted by thoughts and feelings, and have forgotten your breath, just come back to the breathing.

There's no need to scold yourself that you wandered away. To scold yourself is to wander away again. Resume counting from one.

As you meditate, all kinds of self-comments may arise: "There I go again" or "I can't do this" or "I'm not very good at this" or even "I'm not sure I'm doing this right." These comments are quite normal. Observe them, and let them go—they will depart, if you let them.

Don't strive for some special state of mind. There is no special state of mind. If you strive for some special state of mind you'll only disturb your mind.

This sitting meditation is not trance. It is not rest. It is not relaxation. It is just awareness of breath, that's all. Gradually, as your concentration increases, you can count just the exhalations, then just the inhalations. Once you can stay with the breath fairly regularly, you can stop counting and follow the breath alone. Beyond these simple instructions, the meditation itself will teach you what it is.

You will gradually learn to sit like a mountain. Though thoughts will arise, they are merely clouds passing by the mountain. The mountain need not be perturbed by clouds. The clouds pass on, and the mountain continues to sit—observing all, grasping at nothing.

People often ask me how long or how often they should sit in meditation. This is up to you. The morning, before the world becomes too stirred up, is a good time. Or evening. Begin by meditating for five minutes. Gradually you can increase. Twenty or thirty minutes is good.

But what is most important here—far more important than how much you meditate—is that you do it with regularity. Your meditation should become an activity you do regularly, like eating and sleeping.

When it's time to eat, just eat. When it's time to sleep, just sleep. When it's time to breathe, just breathe. And when it's time to meditate, just meditate. This is more important to establish than "how much?" (I don't know how much. Not too much, but some.)

Meditating with others is helpful because they will reflect you; they will help you *see* yourself. But, more than that, meditation with others offers support and encouragement for the long haul. It's not always so easy to establish a meditation practice on your own.

As Shunryu Suzuki says in *Zen Mind, Beginner's Mind*, when you practice meditation, don't try to stop your thinking. Just attend to this moment, stay with the breath, and let it stop by itself.

Give yourself permission to have thoughts. When you're disturbed by your thinking it tends to augment itself and go faster and louder. The more you try to control it, the more it will gain in strength. Give your mind a lot of space and it quiets down; try to control, quiet, or constrict it, and it goes wild. We only need to notice what's happening, and ease off. Let the thinking stop by itself; it will if you leave it alone.

Thoughts, feelings, and emotions come and go in the mind. But they don't stay. If you play with them, or prod them, or develop them, they hang on. They start to branch into other thoughts. That's what the mind does when it's not being attended to.

When you sit and follow your breath, you'll *see* just how busy your mind really is.

Your breath is a unique object for meditation because it resides right at the boundary between inside and outside, between you and the outside world.

If you use any other object for meditation—whether a visual object, or a sound, or a thought—you'll not get past the basic duality. It's still business as usual. There's still that thing "out there," and there's still you. There's still dispositions of mind. There's still longing and loathing, pain and confusion. There's still duhkha.

By setting your attention here, on this supposed boundary, gradually, you can *see* this boundary dissolve. In fact, you can *see* for yourself that there never was any boundary between inside and outside, self and other, in the first place.

You can't approach meditation as business as usual. In meditation, if it's truly meditation, what we're doing is not for the sake of anything. It's done wholly for its own sake. In other words, it's useless. Ordinary "useful" activity is caught up in calculation and weighing and pricing and evaluating. Meditation has nothing to do with any of these.

Don't expect to get anything from meditation—including enlightenment. If you really want enlightenment, just notice what *thus*—Mind—actually is. Notice that a grasping mind is the antithesis of what you say you want.

If meditation were just another activity—our usual activity of trying to get, trying to change, trying to control, trying to bring about—then what's the point of doing it? It's more of what we always do, and repeatedly suffer from. Meditation is not trying to do anything. Dogen notes that when you practice *right meditation*, you

> cease from practice based on intellectual understanding, pursuing words and following after speech, and learn the backward step that turns your light inwardly to illuminate your self. Body and mind of themselves will drop away, and your original face will be manifest. If you want to attain *thusness,* you should practice *thusness* without delay.

If we taste Reality, we must engage it directly—not merely think, speculate, theorize, and discuss it.

The buddha-dharma is not an armchair philosophy, but a thoroughgoing practice. There's no point in meditating just to get the idea of it. Useless though it is, *right meditation* is the very activity that works on the deep, aching needs of the heart. Do *right meditation* even though it's useless. Do it for no purpose. Do it for its own sake. In fact, there is no other way. If you have the least gaining idea, you are not fully engaged. You are not practicing *right meditation*.

Right meditation is where everything is alive—where we neither create nor manipulate, neither possess nor obsess, neither try nor fail.

9
Freedom

There are two kinds of knowledge and two types of views. One consists of beliefs, opinions, conjectures—having an idea of something. It's an intellectual grasping of concepts. This is how we commonly think of knowledge.

But this not true *knowing*. In fact, the natural results of relying on mere conceptual knowledge are fear, discomfort, and confusion—in short, duhkha.

We think that our beliefs and ideas can be relied on to give us satisfaction. But if we examine the effects they have on us we'll discover that, at best, they only temporarily satisfy us. In fact, they're actually our primary sources of anxiety and fear, because they're always subject to contradiction and doubt.

By their very nature, all our ideas and beliefs are frozen views—fragments of Reality, separated from the Whole. In other words, because we rely on what we think (conception), rather than on what we *see* (perception), there's unrest in our mind. Underneath it all, we're uneasy—and, furthermore, we *know* it.

The fact is, we are already enlightened, even now. We *know* Truth. We just habitually overlay our direct experience of Truth with thoughts—with beliefs and opinions and ideas. We pile them all into our conceptual frame, not recognizing the consequences of what we're doing.

The problem is not so much that we do this. In fact, we can hardly help but conceptualize. I couldn't write this book, and you couldn't read it, if we didn't conceptualize. The real problem is that we are caught by our concepts. We don't have to grant them power or accuracy or validity that they don't have. We simply need to recognize that our concepts are not Reality.

The mistake we make, over and over again, is to automatically posit something in our thoughts, without realizing what we've done. And then we run away with our idea, thinking we've captured some aspect of Reality.

What we overlook is that underneath the ground of our beliefs, opinions, and concepts is a boundless sea of uncertainty. The concepts we cling to are like tiny boats tossed about in the middle of a vast ocean. We stand on our beliefs and ideas thinking they're solid, but in fact, they (and we) are on shifting seas. Any ideas or beliefs we hold in our minds are necessarily set against other ideas and beliefs. Thus we cannot help but experience doubt.

This is the deep end of duhkha—existential angst. It's the realization that beneath all our ideas there's profound, unremovable doubt. In the very moment that we overlay our actual, direct experience with conceptual thought, doubt is right there, forever wedded to it.

To see separate, distinct forms is to conceptualize. This doesn't refer only to ideas and thoughts. Physical objects—a cup, a book, even the light falling on this page—are still conceptual. They're still things that we've framed in our minds, separated out from the Whole, and contrasted against everything else. We can talk about them; we can use them; we can manipulate them. We can seek them out, long for them, or push them away. But we shouldn't take these conceptualized, frozen, separated-out objects for Reality. That's where we go wrong. That's where we give rise to duhkha.

The biggest mistake we make in confusing a concept with Reality is in making that nearest and dearest and most fundamental distinction: the separation of self and other. "I am over here, and over there is a world external to me." Unquestioningly believing this to be a full and accurate description of Reality, we ignore immediate experience and seek for things—comfort, happiness, meaning—"out there." "Go for it," we say. (And our confusion remains undiminished even when we seek such things "in here.")

We even turn enlightenment into such an object. But in doing so, we fail to see that we've made it just another concept, another idea, another item to go after—something quite ordinary and illusory.

But if we look closely at our immediate experience, we simply cannot find such a division. Indeed, the harder we look, the more absurd and impossible such a distinction becomes.

As we've seen, there is a second type of view, what the Buddha called *right view*. *Right view* is not a concept or belief. In fact, it's no particular thing at all. *Right view* is simply *seeing* Reality as it is, here and now, moment after moment. It's relying on bare attention—naked awareness of what is before conceptual thought arises. It's relying on what we actually experience rather than on what we think.

If we are to ever find certitude—real *knowledge* that is beyond all doubt and misunderstanding—it's clearly not going to come from our vying concepts and beliefs. Rather, true *knowledge* must appear before all our ideas and opinions. In other words, it's nothing other than immediate, direct experience of the world in and of itself. True *knowledge* is *seeing thus*.

Seeing thus is the unshakable ground we long for simply because it cannot be doubted. Herein lies freedom of mind. And herein lies fearlessness as well.

With the two types of views there are two kinds of minds. As human beings, we all have what we could call ordinary minds— the mind that you've always assumed you've had. It's a calculating mind, a discriminating mind, a fragmented mind. It's the mind of ordinary consciousness, the mind of self and other. We generally think of it as "my mind."

But there's another mind that is unborn, ungrown, and uncon-ditioned. Unlike "your mind," it's unbound, for there is nothing beyond it. To this Mind, there is no "other mind."

This Mind is nothing other than the Whole. It's simply *thus*, the fabric of the world itself—the ongoing arising and falling away that are matter, energy, and events.

Speaking of this Mind, the great Chinese Zen master Huang Po said,

> All buddhas and ordinary people are just One Mind.
> . . . This Mind is beyond all measurements, names, oppositions: this very being is It; as soon as you stir your mind you turn away from It.

This Mind is self-evident—it's always switched on, so to speak. We can—and, in fact, we do—*see* It in every moment. If we would only refrain from stirring our minds (rest our frontal lobes, as my Zen teacher used to say) and let our conceptualizing die down, like the ripples on a pond after the stirring wind has ceased, we would realize—we would *know*—Mind directly.

Our intent need only be to be awake. Yet this must not be a goal as we ordinarily think of it. It's not some end that we should (or even can) strive for or work toward as such. That's why this prac-tice is radically different from everything else we do or can do. When we *see* Reality for what it is, we can't pretend to play the games of reaching, striving, or arriving anymore. You can't get to *seeing*; when you are fully engaged in this moment, this is *see-ing*. Here there isn't any doubt, there isn't any fear, there isn't any existential angst. There are no overwhelming questions such as

"Where do I go after I die?" because it becomes clear that such questions, doubts, fears, and anxieties are based on buying into an illusion—the self.

At the close of the second millennium, it's becoming harder and harder for us to find meaning in our lives. We've seen through too many of our old stories. Religion doesn't grip most people today as it once did. Though a lot of people mouth it, and still desperately cling to it, underneath it all "God" doesn't seem to be the final answer for many of us.

We don't really live as if we believe in God. Still, in desperation, we swing between the twin perils of cynicism and dogmatism. We continue to run to this or that to inject meaning into our lives.

We don't easily understand that we create this problem of meaninglessness ourselves through our deluded thinking. If we could *just see* this moment for what it is, meaninglessness would never arise in the first place. It's in our very trying to define and arrange things for ourselves—trying to identify and assign meanings to things—that we end up creating a world that is ultimately meaningless.

Whatever we hold up as "the meaning of life" will ultimately show itself to be hollow, or false, or contradictory. Yet we keep digging in that same bag, continuing to search fruitlessly for a conceptual explanation. Either that or we fall into despair.

We've tried this, we've tried that, we've tried the next thing, and the next. We've become sophisticated, jaded. After all our searching, all the philosophy and science that we've labored on for centuries, it's becoming very hard to find a story we can buy.

Liberation of mind is realizing that we don't need to buy any story at all. It's realizing that before our confused thought, there actually is Reality. We can *see* it. All we have to do is learn to fully engage in this moment as it has come to be. For this, the eight-fold path points the way.

The deep, hollow ache of the heart arises from a life in search of meaning. But it's by our very desire to find meaning that we create meaninglessness. The very idea of looking for purpose and meaning arises from our deluded thought. When we actually *see* Reality for what it is, all questions of meaning are transcended, and we're free to engage the world as it actually is.

Joseph Campbell said we short-circuit religious experience by putting it into concept. It's true: much of religious teaching is hammered onto conceptual frames. This is as true of Buddhism as it is of any other religion.

If we would awaken, however, we must notice the framework upon which we've attached everything. Ultimately, if we truly seek a free mind, even this eightfold path—even Buddhism itself—must not be clung to. We shouldn't make the buddha-dharma into something holy, something to put up on a gilded pedestal in a prominent place.

This path simply reminds us of how we're engaged in the world. It's like the raft that carries us to the opposite shore. We use it to a point, then leave it behind. Once the stream is crossed, we leave the raft for someone else. We don't need to lug it around. It will only burden us.

Part Three

FREE MIND

10

The Way We Are

The time of the Buddha was one of great philosophical confusion, much like our time today. Many different religious
ideas and systems were offered, discussed, and followed.
One idea that had been developing for centuries was the existence
of a metaphysical self called the *atman*. The atman was thought
to be eternal. The people who believed this theory of an eternal
self or soul were thus known as eternalists.

The eternalists' theory says that there's an everlasting core in
each of us, temporarily housed in a body that is subject to death
and decay. This eternal self survives the corruptible body beyond
death. With such a soul theory in place, other attendant notions
emerged as well, including the idea of a creator God.

Soon an opposite notion arose to counter the atman theory. A
group of philosophers in ancient India, known as materialists,
argued that there's no such entity as the atman—an eternal self or
soul—within humankind at all. The death of the body is the death

of the psycho-physical being, they said. The whole person dies and decays along with the body. All that remains after death is just matter, a functionless body, which soon decays. The materialists' idea was that while matter is eternal, there's no enduring self.

Though such theories were debated long ago in India, we find the same ideas being tossed about today. Indeed, even after centuries of serious debate and ballyhoo, the same fight still rages.

And the same essential questions continue to arise. What am I? Why am I here? What does it mean to be human? How did I come to be? What happens to me when I die? Do I go on after death? Will I ever be able to find conclusive answers to these questions? This is the human problem—the problem of being. It drives us, one by one, generation after generation, to pain and sorrow.

This is the real, underlying problem all our suffering stems from, a problem we can't dismiss. The discomfort of confusion, the agony and horror of being intelligent enough to know that we will die, the realization that everything we believe and everyone we know will come to an end—how can we deal with these? How can we deal with this profound problem of being, without resorting to speculation and belief?

We are deluded about self. In one form or another, we're very confused about this perennial idea of the atman, the eternal self or soul. Do we all have one, or don't we? Whether we latch on to "yes," "no," or even "I don't know," what we're left with is disturbing, to say the least. Try to defend any of these positions and you'll find it impossible. Any answer we come up with fails to still the deep, persistent ache of the heart. In fact, each of the three options leads us inevitably to still more frightening and confusing prospects.

If we say "yes," then we've put everything on the belief that the self or atman is the center of Reality. If we believe in such an everlasting self, it's tantamount to proclaiming that we have existed before all else came into being. We may as well fancy ourselves as being the cause of all creation.

Perhaps this is not what we mean by "eternal," but only that the self exists now, but will not die. But then how, when, and by whom was this self created? Did it exist before the Big Bang? (Was there a Big Bang?) Will it cease to exist after the human race dies out? After the Earth is enveloped by the sun a few billion years from now? After the entire universe contracts into a tiny, incredibly hot, dense point? Or after the entire universe expands and cools into a "heat death"?

Furthermore, if we buy the notion of a creator, beyond the bickering this belief inevitably engenders, we face the problem of determining what, if anything, might be expected of us by such a being—another point of controversy. We also have the problem of forever pleasing and protecting ourselves within this world that leaves us with such enormous, urgent, and yet unanswerable questions. In other words, we still face this same, unresolvable problem.

If we say "no, there is no self," then our mind starts spinning in another direction. If there's no self, then who or what is it that's experiencing our lives? What is it that senses and feels and expresses itself? If all is just matter and energy, how can we account for perception and consciousness? Why isn't the whole universe lifeless and consciousless? What is it that's asking all these questions? And what is it that's feeling this deep heartache and confusion? If we say "no," we're faced with the problem of being intelligent creatures in a meaningless universe. What could possibly be more unsettling than this?

If we say, in all honesty, "I don't know," how long can we go on without a definitive answer to this all-important question? How long before our persistent heartache, our existential confusion, and our despair become unendurable?

And if we simply turn away from the question, how long before our denial crumbles under the weight of duhkha? Will we be able to continue to ignore or deny the question on our deathbed?

Beyond the profoundly disturbing nature of these questions, the fact is that there is no evidence in our actual experience to support any of these positions—including "I don't know." If we take any of these positions, we do so as an act of faith, a faith that is itself both profoundly disturbing and highly susceptible to doubt.

It was this profound problem that the Buddha set out to clarify and demolish. And demolish it he did—totally and without question.

The resolution lies with neither "yes" nor "no." But nor does it lie in "don't know," because the fact of the matter is that we do *know*. We're just not very good at recognizing what it is that we actually *know*.

The Buddha *saw* through this seemingly unanswerable question. What he found was a *view* that has no counter, a *view* that appears the same to all who *see*. In doing so, he understood that both the eternalists' view ("there is a self") and the materialists' view ("there is no self, only matter") were extreme and unverifiable accounts of Reality.

In the eternalists' group of views it was denied that all things come to an end. The Buddha, relying on direct experience alone, not only found no evidence of beginnings or endings, he could find no evidence of any separate, persisting thing that could have a beginning or end.

But this is not to say that there's no experience, there is only matter—the view the materialists took. The Buddha rejected this nihilistic view as well. He regarded it as extreme, since it didn't account for the presence of consciousness—a presence which is, of course, self-evident.

The buddha-dharma is called the middle way because it rejects any extreme view, what the Buddha called "frozen views." These are views that attempt to wrap Reality into nice, neat packages.

We're strongly inclined to hold tight to certain views since they give us a sense of solidity under our feet. Unfortunately, they simply can't hold Reality, and thus they always leave us susceptible to doubt and confusion—duhkha. Most of the views we hold might not seem extreme to us at first glance, but the more closely we examine them, the more extreme (and absurd) they become.

All the views we hold (and hold dear) appear in sets of two or more. Most often, they appear as pairs of opposites: pro and con, Western and Eastern, liberal and conservative, dualistic and non-dualistic. For example, "People are basically good" posits an ultimate quality of goodness, then attributes this quality to every member of our species. As soon as it's offered, however, it immediately invites a counter view: "People are basically evil." This is essentially the same view, but leaning in the opposite direction.

Can you *see*, based on your immediate experience alone, that neither of these views point to Reality? They are both concepts—attempts to freeze Reality into something hard, fast, solid, and packaged.

Review your own experience. Do you find a specific thing called Goodness that provides the primary motivation for everyone you've met? What about Evil? Do you find that Evil exists as a specific thing, and that it serves as the biggest motivation in every human being's life?

Inherent Goodness and inherent Evil are both frozen views—notions, concepts. They don't refer to anything in actual experience. This is not to say that people don't act in ways that can be called good or evil, but only that inherent Goodness and inherent Evil are conceptual inventions—philosophical objects of our own creation. Both of these views fail to point to Reality. Reality is far more fluid than either of these extreme views is capable of indicating. Indeed, any such frozen view is, by definition, extreme—and, therefore, incapable of reflecting Reality.

What we generally fail to appreciate is that it's simply by our holding onto a specific view—believing in it, relying on it, clinging to it—that it becomes frozen and extreme.

The Buddha repudiated all such views. Because they are by nature conceptual, they attempt to freeze the world into solid, separate entities, whether those entities are Goodness, Evil, selves, non-selves, books, light, enlightenment, Buddhism, or any thing or thought whatsoever. Of course, all such attempts fail. The world of experience simply isn't frozen. Reality won't be condensed into concepts. Our immediate, direct experience bears this out.

Imagine that someone comes up to you and asks, "Are people basically good?" You might answer: "No, not in my experience."

The person responds, "Oh, I see. So people are basically evil." What would you say now?

You'd have to answer again, "No, not in my experience."

Now imagine that your questioner gets very agitated. "What do you mean? You can't have it both ways! If people aren't basically good, they must be basically evil! You're contradicting yourself!"

But, of course, you're not contradicting yourself at all. You're simply *seeing* beyond the duality in which your questioner is caught. You can *see* that human beings are too complex and fluid to be basically either good or evil. Indeed, they are too complex and fluid to be "basically" anything at all in particular. You can *see* Reality past the conceptualizing, past the questioner's frozen view.

This is precisely what the Buddha did in relation to concepts of selfhood. The Buddha *saw* that both the assertion of an eternal self (atman) and the denial of such a self (*anatman*) are frozen views that do not account for actual experience. They are merely concepts we construct out of our longing, loathing, and ignorance.

Many people understand that the Buddha denied the existence of an everlasting, unchanging self. And they're right. Buddha did *see* through the extreme view of the eternalists. What is less understood, however, is that the Buddha also denied the opposite extreme view, that of the materialists, or nihilists. What is worse, many people think, "The Buddha said there is no self; therefore Buddhism is a religion of nihilism." This is like thinking, "Since you don't believe that God is a handsome, elderly gentleman with a long, white beard who lives in the clouds, you must be an atheist."

It's very easy to get caught up in such dualities without realizing that we're doing so. To deny a concept is not to embrace its opposite. When you say no to the question "Is the boogeyman still hiding in your closet?" you're not saying that the boogeyman has gone out for the day. You are denying the validity of the question itself.

The Buddha denied the question "Is there a self or not?" in just the same way. The Buddha *saw* that neither option—neither extreme—reflects actual experience. In fact, the question itself pertains no more to Reality than does the question "Is the boogeyman still hiding in your closet?" They are both based on totally unsubstantiated assumptions about Reality.

When we first ask what the term "self" actually refers to, confusion sets in immediately. If we look up the word "self" in a dictionary, we find that it's generally defined as "not other." What is "other," then? "Not self." This doesn't get us anywhere.

We can *see* that the term "self" refers to the existence of a supposed entity that doesn't change. When you say, "When I was six years old, I was in first grade," the "I" refers to something that must have been the same at the age of six as it is now. If it isn't the same, then what in the world does "I" refer to? And if the entity is the same, what's the same about it? Its appearance? Its memory? The cells that make up its body? (Indeed, what now does "it" refer to?) All of these have changed drastically over the years, and continue to change now. To assume the existence of a self, an "I," is to assume the existence of something that has not changed, that has remained itself through all these intervening years. And if the thing in question—the "I"—has changed, in what manner can it still be itself? To change would mean it has become something else.

It's impossible for anything to remain itself and yet change. But this is precisely the thing we can't find—a self that doesn't change. For that matter, as we have seen, we can't find anything that doesn't change. In fact, we can't find any solid thing at all.

Whatever you can point to—a physical thing, a person, a thought, an emotion—all are without self. All of them change. Even memory shows nothing but flux and change. There's nothing, no component of mind or body, that isn't in constant flux. Whether we talk about our physical body, or the bodies of the natural world—animals, plants, stones, lakes, raindrops, stars— or the objects of our purposeful world—chairs, windows, milk cartons, and sewing needles—we find nothing but flux and change. Every atom, every minuscule part of the universe, is nothing other than movement and change. The same is true of our mental experience, our feelings, thoughts, and images.

It's an indisputable fact of experience—of our direct, immediate perception—that all things are empty of self. Yet we think and believe and act and hope otherwise. It's by holding onto this notion of self—and we hold it most dear—that we live in defiance of Reality.

This is the means by which we suffer, and suffer greatly. It hurts to defy Reality.

But don't we need the concept of a self in order to explain experience? How can there be experience without a self to have that experience? The Truth is that we don't need such an explanation, and that's all the self is: an explanation of experience.

Reality needs no explanation. In fact, Reality is precisely what doesn't need an explanation, since any explanation removes us from direct experience to the realm of concepts.

Reality is simply *thus*—immediate, direct experience, prior to any ideas or explanations at all. To explain Reality is to box it up and cart it away. It's to ignore the territory for the map.

The Buddha *saw* that the notion of a self is not required to account for actual experience. He *saw* that the self is merely a concept formed out of our desire to get a handle on things rather than accept our experience as Real but ungraspable.

Of course, the term "I" can—indeed, must—be used in conventional ways in order for us to talk with one another, and write and read books, and so on. But it's not a very accurate term.

When the Buddha spoke of individuals, he often used a different term: "stream." Imagine a stream flowing—constantly moving and changing, always different from one moment to the next. Most of us see ourselves as corks floating in a stream, persisting things moving along in the stream of time. But this is yet another frozen view. According to this view, everything in the stream changes except the cork. While we generally admit to changes in our body, our mind, our thoughts, our feelings, our understandings, and our beliefs, we still believe, "I myself don't change. I'm still me. I'm an unchanging cork in an ever-changing stream." This is precisely what we believe the self to be—something that doesn't change.

The fact is, however, that there are no corks in the stream. There is only stream. What we conceptualize as "cork" is also stream. We are like music. Music, after all, is a type of stream.

Music exists only in constant flow and flux and change. Once the movement stops, the music is no more. It exists not as a particular thing, but as pure coming and going with no thing that comes or goes.

Look at this carefully. If this is true—how a stream exists, how music exists, and how we exist—*see* how it is that when we insert the notion of "I" we've posited some little, solid entity that floats along, not as stream, but like a cork in a stream. We see ourselves as solid corks, not as the actual stream we are.

If we are the stream, what is it that experiences the flux, the flow, the change? The Buddha *saw* that there is no particular thing that is having an experience. There is experience, but no experiencer. There is perception, but no perceiver. There is consciousness, but no self that can be located or identified.

We experience duhkha because, not *seeing* the true nature of things, we long for something permanent, something that doesn't change. Yet our actual experience provides nothing but change.

Because of this basic confusion, we long for something we can get our hands on. We want to hold it, to cling to it. What we love, we want to last. What we hate, we want to get rid of forever.

Because of change, however, what we hate can't be forever kept away, but returns. Because of change, what we love doesn't remain, but surely fades. If we'd only relax, we'd notice that, because of change, what we love continues to appear, and what we hate never lasts forever. We'd also observe that there's no abiding self to be either pleased or damaged.

This is what we have to *see*—that all is flux and movement and flow. It's because we believe that there's some static being in the midst of all of this—an imagined permanence we call "I"—that we suffer duhkha.

Sometimes, when people first hear of this teaching, they feel a sense of unease or fear. Indeed, for some of us, it's the most terrifying thing we've ever contemplated. "You mean I don't actually exist? This sense of myself is an illusion? I'm not really here at all?" It sounds like a death sentence. Worse, it sounds as if we're already dead and don't even know it. Why would anyone want to awaken to the Reality that they're not even here in the first place?

This fear arises from holding an extreme view, the counter view to "I am possessed of a self." It's assuming the existence of a self, then trembling at the thought of having this assumed entity taken away.

If it's merely being assumed in the first place, we should realize that there's nothing being taken away, either. The self that we don't have is like the boogeyman that's not in your closet. It's not that the boogeyman has stepped away. There never was a boogeyman in the first place.

Our situation is like that of a little boy I once saw going in for an X-ray. It seemed he might have broken his arm, and a medical technician was leading him to a room with a great big X-ray machine sitting in the middle of it. When the technician opened the door, the little boy looked at the big machine and cringed. He had probably gone through a lot already—and now he faced this big, scary machine.

142

The technician saw his discomfort and asked softly, "Are you afraid of that big machine?"

The little boy nodded shyly.

To put him at ease, she said, "Well, it won't hurt you. It's just going to take your picture."

We're afraid in much the same way as this little boy. We don't understand consciousness, just as the boy didn't understand the X-ray machine. Naturally we're terrified that whatever it is we're about to confront, it's going to hurt.

But I'll speak the X-ray technician's part here and tell you it won't hurt. The fact of the matter is that it's not awakening to Truth that hurts—quite the opposite. It's our defiance of Reality, brought about by ignoring our own direct experience of Reality, that hurts us.

All we have to do to alleviate such fear is to consider that Reality already is what it is. If it happens to be that all things are without an abiding self, then what's the difference between that and now? In other words, what's there to be afraid of?

It's not as if, when you *see*, the world winks out of existence. If you're simply *seeing* Reality, Reality is not going to change through your perception of it. Reality remains Reality. You will simply *see* it for what it is—which is nothing in particular. Waking up to Truth isn't painful. It's through our confusion about Reality that we suffer, not through Reality itself.

Although the primary enduring entity we imagine to exist is our self, selfhood can apply to any thing or thought. Take this book, for example. We imagine it as a distinct, separate object, existing totally on its own. We conceive that it is a particular thing that came into existence at a certain time in the past, and that it now endures and will crumble to dust and pass out of existence sometime in the future. And then we say, "That's the end of the book."

But, as we've already considered, we can't find any definitive beginning or end to this book—or to anything, really. To think that we do is to lock onto the idea of a persistent, abiding, thing. Even now, if you pay close attention to immediate experience, you don't actually find any abiding thing you can point to as "this book." Like all things, what we're calling "this book" is only change and flux.

For instance, the book you're holding now doesn't appear at all like the closed book you picked up a while ago to read. You say, "That's because I picked it up and opened it." But, that's change.

The problem is, what does "it" in the phrase "I picked it up and opened it" refer to? There's nothing static and unchanging— nothing remaining itself, in other words—that's being referred to here at all. The "it" we assume we refer to is only a mental construction.

We know from modern science that the dynamic process we're provisionally referring to as "this book" is a collection of rapidly moving molecules. Each one in itself is nothing but ferment, and all the molecules continuously interchange their electrons with other molecules and atoms. In short, this book is nothing but constant change itself. It's flowing stream, not solid cork.

Just as "this book" is only a mental construction, an idea, so it is with anything we conceive to exist on its own.

As we've seen, once we've fixed on the idea of a universe full of separate, unchanging, persisting things (as is our habit), we've already created the notion that each thing must have gotten started at some moment in the past. We also necessarily conceive that each thing must die, must one day come to an end. And when the thing in question is the imagined "I," this prospect naturally terrifies us.

But if we pay very close attention to our actual experience, we'll notice that we don't find anything like this occurring—ever! All we ever find is the arising and ceasing of the world as it has come to be now. When you snap your fingers it's already gone. All that persists is *thus*. *Thus* is not an object of mind but Mind Itself. There is only this eternal arising and ceasing—but there's no thing that comes or goes. This is our actual experience from moment to moment. If we would *just see*, just rely on perception alone, we'd *see* the ongoing arising and ceasing of the world as it has come to be *now*—and all our confusion about the nature of existence would vanish instantly.

Our only hope of cutting off duhkha at its source is not through more exploration, theorizing, or partying, but through learning to *see* directly just how we're chronically confused.

11

Can't Pin "Me" Down

It seems that it has always been our lot to experience duhkha. If we're human, we habitually conceptualize our experience, thus conceiving a self. The fact that this self 1) is unlocatable, 2) contradicts direct experience, and 3) is quite literally impossible doesn't do much to weaken the sense we generally have that it exists somewhere inside us, if not in our bodies, then at least in our minds.

We should notice, however, that once we have a firm belief in self, we can't account for our experience at all, and consciousness must remain totally mysterious.

Furthermore, we suffer deep existential angst because we misinterpret actual experience. Instead of simply attending to what we actually perceive, we conceive a self and then quiver in our boots, afraid that it might be taken away, injured, or made unhappy.

Of course, we can't just drop our notion of a self as we would remove a garment. It's a rather compelling illusion. The only way we'll *see* what's illusory about it is to learn to take note of our actual experience, and *see* just how it differs from our thoughts and concepts about it. Once it's *seen* that the "I" cannot be found the mind is free and is no longer afraid.

It's very much like no longer fearing the boogeyman. As children, our fear of this fellow may have been strong and real. Then we matured, and the fear disappeared. Not because we found ways to keep the boogeyman out of our closets with chants and rituals, not because we found effective ways to barricade our closets at night, not because we learned to get our minds off the boogeyman by distracting and entertaining ourselves all day (until night falls, anyway). It disappeared because we awoke to Reality. The boogeyman never existed in the first place. We saw that the terrifying creature that we had feared for years existed only in our imaginations.

So it is with our sense of self. The issues of what a self is, how long it will last, what will happen when our bodies die and decay and our consciousness flickers off, are all based not on what we actually *see* but on what we imagine. The horrendous issues we've always feared turn out to exist only in our thoughts, concepts, and imaginations, not in Reality.

By attending carefully to our actual, direct experience, each of us can *see* this directly. And when we do *see* this, we're released from far more than the irrational fears of a childhood fantasy. We're free of the deep fear and horror that have relentlessly plagued humankind.

Each one of us can awaken from this pain without resorting to stories or gimmicks. We can finally *see* that we've been distressed and worried over an illusion.

We've *seen* that the abiding self or soul we commonly assume we are is an illusion, a figment of the imagination. Perhaps we've also begun to understand that we conceive all the innumerable aspects of the world in the same manner. Rather than *see* the wind, or waves—or a stream or a cup or a book—as the constant flux that each is, we imagine them to be solid, persisting, separate, unchanging things.

We attribute this "thingness" to them in the same way that we attribute selfhood to human beings. Instead of *seeing* the thoroughgoing motion, flux, and flow of experience, we imagine a vast proliferation of innumerable, separated things. In short, we grant selfhood to whatever we find "out there."

Then we make another error. Just as we conceive of a self and counter this notion with a non-self, so also are we taken in by another set of opposing concepts—existence and non-existence. We get repeatedly caught in this duality, unwilling to *see* that, like self and not-self, both are phantoms created by consciousness. These concepts (like any concept) simply don't capture Reality.

The Buddha expressed this situation eloquently:

> This world . . . is generally inclined towards two [views]: existence and non-existence. To them who perceive with right wisdom the uprising of the world as it has come to be, the notion of non-existence in the world does not occur. . . . To them who perceive with right wisdom the ceasing of the world as it has come to be, the notion of existence in the world does not occur.

When we *just see*—when we rely on perception alone, before the arising of any concept of some enduring, unchanging self, separate and apart from everything else—then the concept of nonexistence doesn't occur. Our belief in non-existence arises only as the result of holding the notion of existence in the first place. It's only because we so thoroughly believe in, and so strongly feel, the sense of "I" and "the world apart from me" that we experience confusion, fear, and trembling.

Conversely, if we perceive with *right wisdom* the ceasing of the world as it has come to be in this moment, if we *see* the fleeting nature of all things without overlaying what we *see* with concepts, then the notion of a permanent self doesn't occur. Though there's still thought and sensation, there's no notion of a permanent self—only peace of mind and fearlessness.

It's the same whether we talk about the arising or ceasing of "me" or of "the world," since both of these illusions occur at once. With perception alone—in the absence of conception—neither the notion of self, nor of a world external to self, occurs. It's only when we posit the concept of existence that we're driven to either of the two wretched extremes of eternalism or nihilism, or to oscillating between them.

As the Buddha pointed out, neither of these conclusions can be derived from our actual experience.

When the Buddha said, "To them who perceive with *right wisdom* . . ." we should understand that this perception is available to all of us right now. We all perceive the same, whether we're a buddha or not. We all perceive Truth and Reality right now. If this were not so, there'd be no hope of awakening.

An ordinary person is simply one who is not awake in this moment; a buddha is a person who is. That's all. The movement of the senses, our sensual experience of the world, is no different for a buddha than it is for anyone else.

What's the difference, then, between a buddha and an ordinary human being? The difference is not in perception. It's in conception. To a buddha—to a person with *right wisdom*—there's no habitual overlaying of perceptual experience with concepts, with ideas, beliefs, notions, pre-formed habits of thought, that are used to explain experience. Thus we all have the capacity to awaken.

Our usual way is to take sense experience—perception—and immediately, before we even know we're doing it, we divide our seamless direct experience into concepts. Then we label these concepts, organize them, and hang them in an elaborate and cherished framework that we have long and laboriously built upon.

A buddha, however, isn't caught by this. When buddhas conceptualize (and they do), they realize what they're doing and aren't taken in by it. After all, it's not conceptualization itself that's the problem, but getting caught up in it, mistaking our concepts for Reality.

The awakened may have thoughts and concepts just like anyone else. The difference is that they're aware that what they actually *see* differs from what they think.

The Buddha called this awareness *right wisdom*.

12

Interdependence

I n our confusion, it can be easy to think that what I have been discussing thus far is abstract, hypothetical, or distant from our practical, everyday lives. This is a great error. We have it completely backward, in fact. If we see Truth and Reality—the arising and ceasing of the world as it has come to be in this moment—then we immediately see that the stuff of our ordinary thought is abstract, concept-ridden, and irrelevant to Truth. The stuff we commonly take for Reality—such as "myself"—is highly conceptual, and thus divorced from Reality. But what is Real and True is immediately perceivable without any abstract thought— any concepts—whatsoever.

How do we account for actual experience without being confused by it? This isn't a mere academic question. It has immediate, practical value, because what arises out of our confusion determines how we treat each other, the planet, and ourselves.

The buddha-dharma encourages us to notice that our commonsense view of things, our basic, background assumptions about ourselves and about the world, is based on a grand illusion. And it can help us pinpoint exactly what the illusion is.

It's like observing the picture of the cow on page 30. At first it looked like nothing but blobs of ink on the page. It didn't make any sense at all. But if you kept looking at it, or returning to it, eventually, all of a sudden, you could see what it is. "Hey! I see it! It's a cow!" *Seeing* is like that.

That's the work we're doing here. But instead of discerning a picture of a static cow, our task is *seeing* Reality.

Consciousness is nothing more that the splitting of Reality into this and that. Consciousness is making distinctions and drawing lines. That is set off "over there," and you're set off "over here." Consciousness divides what is otherwise the direct experience of a seamless Whole into the world of multiplicity, the world of space and time. (Or, rather, it appears to divide up the Whole. The Whole of course remains whole.)

Because of consciousness, the universe appears "out there," loaded with stuff. And, likewise, because of consciousness, "here I am" as well.

We engage in conceptualizing to clarify, to understand, to find certitude. We vainly try to somehow express Truth in language. If we can pin it down, we think, then we'll have it. Yet what we attempt to get through grasping—peace of mind, the lack of confusion—is lost by our very attempt to grasp Truth and Reality.

How long does it take for us to *see* that we go nowhere with this process? It's the perennial issue—we teach uncertainty, doubt, and meaninglessness to our children, all in the name of "truth." Thus we give rise to duhkha for ourselves and for each other. And it just goes on, generation after generation, the continuation of greed, anger, and ignorance.

We have packaged and repackaged and repackaged again our thoughts and beliefs, constantly organizing and reorganizing them. But by now we *know* that we will never touch Reality that way. Reality is in *seeing*, in direct perception alone. No means are necessary. Truth and Reality are simply not to be found in any way we frame our thoughts. Indeed, the more we search for Truth among our thoughts and beliefs, the more subject to doubt we become.

It's this very grasping, this holding, this getting things and thoughts into a conceptual frame—and the longing and loathing that accompany such grasping—that trouble us so. Anything that can be grasped must of necessity depend on other things for their validity. Hence, they are doubtful and perplexing. Doubt is just the flipside of belief. As soon as we look to belief, doubt arises with it. The two are as inseparable as the dualities of self and other, or existence and non-existence. The moment that we hold some solidified idea about Reality—rather than relying on direct perception of the world—we inevitably give rise to anxiety and fear.

In short, duhkha is not something foisted upon us. We create our own suffering and confusion.

155

When we cease to be bound by our concepts, our paradigms, our grasping, or our inclinations of mind, our doubt ceases as well, because our *knowledge* is no longer dependent on anything beyond immediate, direct experience.

Seeing doesn't require conception, language, or memory. "Herein," said the Buddha, "*knowledge* is not other-dependent." Herein lies freedom.

There can be no secret teachings regarding Truth and Reality. Truth is here for all to *see*. We're fully equipped to *just see*, right now.

Nagarjuna, the brilliant Buddhist philosopher of second-century India, wrote,

> Those who do not understand the distinction between [the] two truths do not understand the profound truth embodied in the Buddha's message.

These two truths are relative truth and Absolute Truth.

Relative truths are the day-to-day things and thoughts we can easily discuss, teach, sell, and conceptualize. These include simple facts—a foot is twelve inches, oranges contain vitamin C, Mount McKinley is in North America. But feet, inches, oranges, rocks, birds, feelings, and thoughts, are themselves also relative truths. Each one depends on a vast multiplicity of other things, other concepts, other relative truths for its existence—an existence which is, of course, one hundred percent conceptual.

Relative truths are the concepts we use to get an easy handle on the world. They help us in our everyday lives with a huge variety of practical matters. But the more closely we look at them, the less Real they show themselves to be.

Nevertheless, relative truths aren't to be avoided. They're not necessarily evil, or harmful, or wrong. Indeed, they're essential. In order to get through the day, we need to know things—telephone numbers, store hours, potatoes, growing seasons, fractions, love, speed limits, how to fasten shoes. We run into trouble when we forget that all these things, thoughts, and feelings are relative—that they are not Real, independent entities at all. They exist only in relation to other things, thoughts, and feelings. When we refer to "this book," that is a relative truth. And we've already seen that the more closely we examine what "this book" is, the more we can't pin it down, and the more the "truth" of it dissipates like a morning mist after sunrise.

Relative truths are why we fight wars, why we fear people who aren't like us, and why we debate the abortion question but come no closer to a resolution of it.

Ultimate Truth, on the other hand, is direct perception. And what is directly perceived (as opposed to conceived) is that no separate, individualized things exist as such. There's nothing to be experienced but this seamless, thoroughgoing relativity and flux.

In other words, there are no particulars, but only *thus*.

Ultimate Truth can't be conceptualized or imagined. You cannot hold Ultimate Truth in your mind at all. You can *see* It. You just can't hold It as an idea.

Ultimate Truth appears the same to all who *see*. It can't be countered or doubted or discounted because it is immediate, direct experience itself. It's not other-dependent. It has no "other." What's ultimately True can't be held in opposition to something else.

We can actually *see* this. We can (and, in fact, we do) *see* for ourselves, right now, Ultimate Truth, and Reality. Our only problem is that we ignore what we *see*.

Ignorance is not the inability to *see*, but the act of ignoring what is really going on in favor of what we imagine. The nature of ignorance is like this. Consider a concave line like the one on this page.

At this point you probably think of the line on this page as concave because that's how I identified it—and, perhaps, because of the way it's oriented on the page. But there's nothing inherently concave about it. It could just as easily be considered convex. Just turn the book upside down. Indeed, if you draw a single concave line, you've also drawn a convex one.

Our state of ignorance is analogous to noting only the concave and not taking into account the convex. We forget—or ignore—the fact that whenever we come up with any concept at all, we simultaneously create one or more opposite concepts. Each relative truth engenders other opposite relative truths. And if we take the opposing concepts for reality, they will inevitably cause misery. Consider this well-known Zen story.

> A monk asked Tung Shan, "When cold and heat come upon us, how can we avoid them?"

Shan said, "Why don't you go to where there is no
cold or heat?"
The monk said, "Where is there no cold or heat?"
Shan said, "When cold, let cold kill you; when hot,
let hot kill you."

If you draw the one, you've drawn the other. If you feel one,
you feel the other. If you identify one, you've identified the
other—and the world "out there" in relation to it.

Reality, of course, is neither concave nor convex, neither cold
nor hot, neither self nor other. If we conceive cold apart from the
rest of Reality—not only apart from heat, but apart from ourselves
as well—we suffer from it.

We ignore Wholeness because we're so fixed on our object—
the thing we've drawn, the thing we feel, the thing we've identified. But we ignore the fact that whatever our object is not is
present as well. By splitting Reality into parts, and then focusing
on the single part, we've tuned out the Whole. We've set ourselves
up for confusion and despair.

A seiche is the kind of wave that forms in a basin or a bathtub
when the water sloshes back and forth. This kind of movement
goes on constantly in our mind when it's occupied with conceptual definitions. We vacillate endlessly between longing and loathing. Our leaning mind, our dispositions and intentions, sends us
back and forth, locked in habitual patterns of thought and action.
This is bondage. This is duhkha.

We tend not to realize the extent to which we make up what
we call the world, that is, the realm of relative truths. We set the
boundaries, we make the definitions. We determine what is good,

what is bad, what ought to be, and what ought not to be—all out of our inclinations of mind. But we seldom recognize the total relativity—the total meaninglessness—of all our defining. We don't see that it's through our obsession with meaning that we create meaninglessness.

But the confusion we find in the world is not actually in the world; rather, it appears as the result of ignoring our own actual experience in favor of relative truth.

What can we do about all this? We can *see* how our mind inclines. And through *seeing,* we can stop.

When buddhas look at the world, they don't *see* solidity. They don't *see* selves. They *see* only flux.

This is not to say that the awakened no longer see forms like the rest of us. They do. But they *see* forms—or, rather, "formness"—as illusory. They *see* that all things arise together. They *see* that the apparent existence of anything is dependent on all that it is not. And they *see* this dependence as nothing other than change and motion themselves.

The Buddha called this phenomena dependent arising. Dependent arising is the formula, "When this arises, that becomes." When the days lengthen, spring flowers bloom. When days shorten, autumn colors appear and leaves fall from the trees. Spring flowers are inseparable from lengthening days; autumn colors are inseparable from days of less and less light. Indeed, spring flowers *are* the longer days; fall colors *are* the shorter days. In Reality, all phenomena work together as a seamless whole.

Dependent arising is not vague, mystical, remote, intellectual stuff. The buddha-dharma is very practical and down-to-earth.

Just pay very close attention to your actual experience, and you'll *see* it for yourself.

Though it's seemingly filled with a multitude of forms, the world as a Whole has no intention, no inclination, no leaning of mind as we do. The Whole generates these apparent forms and patterns in a way our willed action cannot. The falling of a leaf from a tree, the flow of a stream, the sound and movement of wind—all these are natural, effortless, wondrous, deeply alive. And all are activities that are unwilled.

Unwilled action, over time, will produce a natural pattern of leaves on the grass. Willed action will not.

Willed actions—actions undertaken by our ordinary minds of longing and loathing—are based on illusions, on concepts. They're born of thinking that "this" and "that" are real, solid, and intrinsically separate—an assumption which sets the stage for the working of will.

But the Whole has no will. It leans neither toward nor away. This doesn't mean that we're incapable of acting in a natural way. We all are. In fact, this is precisely how a buddha acts—out of the Whole.

Our chronic problem has to do with intention. Because we ignore the Whole, we're taken in by the parts. We're seduced by the objects of our consciousness—our concepts—and, with longing and loathing, greed and anger, our minds start to lean toward and away. This is duhkha.

There's a way out of this dilemma. It's simply to watch your own mind, and *know* when it's leaning.

Earlier we visualized a leaf falling from a tree. We "saw" it land within a pattern of leaves upon the ground. While it's a pattern we cannot replicate by a simple act of will, nature has no trouble producing random patterns at all. What controls the placement of leaves in an utterly random way, yielding a pattern that is so strikingly beautiful? The Whole, of course.

We can't know all the details of the Whole. For example, if we knew everything about the weather system on this planet, we would be able to accurately predict the weather over an extended period. But to do this we would have to know every little detail, right down to the positions and movements of each atom—and, of course, we can't do that. Natural systems, like our planet's weather, are and will always be under the control of the intentionless Whole.

But while we can't know the details of the Whole, the fact is that we—each one of us—already *know* the Whole itself. There's nothing mysterious about Reality—*thus*—at all. It is ever-present, clear, and obvious. Rather than trying to figure something out, trying to *see*, or trying to reunite with the Whole, all we have to do is to notice whether our mind is leaning or not.

When you notice that your mind is caught up in longing and loathing—leaning toward or away from something—don't try to stop it from leaning. As we've seen, trying to make a leaning mind stop leaning is just another form of leaning. ("I really want not to have a leaning mind.") Just be aware when your mind is leaning, and realize what leaning of mind actually is. With practice and attention to this moment, your mind will, of its own accord, lean less.

As a leaf lands in the yard, so your mind will straighten up in a most natural way, and accord with Mind Itself—that is, the Whole.

To *see* doesn't mean to initiate a program of inaction. People often misunderstand this. To act, or not to act, is not the question. The question is whether or not we're awake.

What we have to do is *see* what's happening in each moment, and base our actions on what we *see*, not on what we think. As Huang Po said,

> The foolish reject what they see, not what they think.
> The wise reject what they think, not what they see.

When we actually *see* what's happening, when we *see* the natural order of things—how things are interconnected, and how events unfold—we'll cease to act in defiance of Reality.

Forget yourself. *See* how your mind is leaning. What sustains us is already in place. We need only stop living in painful ignorance of it.

Forget these words, and start noticing if your mind is leaning—showing preferences, making calculations, trying to bring about, trying to push away.

Liberation of mind doesn't result by acting out of a desire to be right, or to do good. That's just another road to duhkha.

Our actions must instead come only out of the desire to be awake.

Our life is like a wheel out of kilter. It's not satisfying. "There's something out there I've got to get. And there's something else out there I've got to keep away from me." This is bondage—this wanting, leaning, craving for something outside ourselves. It comes from that illusory vision of seeing our selves as separate and real. The only choice we have in life is whether or not to be awake.

Our job is to *see* where things don't make sense, when things aren't working out, where life is utterly baffling. We must note what a profound ache in the heart we feel and realize what it is we don't know. We must *see* our ignorance and confusion.

There isn't anything "out there" that ultimately satisfies. There isn't anything "out there" that we must acquire or repel. In fact, there isn't any "out there" at all. Nothing enters or leaves the Mind.

Once we realize what actually goes on in a leaning mind, we'll no longer crave what had great attraction for us in our ignorance. We'll refrain from plunging ourselves into duhkha with the same natural ease that we refrain from putting our hand into a burning flame. We will no longer do what we can *see* will be painful.

When your mind is not leaning, it's none other than Whole Mind.

Attend to immediate experience. Cultivate your mind in meditation. Become familiar with the workings and leanings of your own mind. You'll be spared a great deal of misery, and ultimately you'll *know* True Freedom.

Open your wisdom eye, and *just see* Whole Mind.

Epilogue
Be a Light Unto Yourself

As his death approached, the Buddha said to those who were gathered around him:

Be a light unto yourself; betake yourselves to no external refuge. Hold fast to the Truth. Look not for refuge to anyone besides yourselves.

You'll not find what satisfies the heartmind in a book, or in a teaching. You'll not find it even in what the Buddha taught.

You won't get Truth from the Buddha, or from a venerated Zen master or lama, or from a priest or monk or nun or teacher or guru. You won't receive Truth—what quiets the deepest ache of the heart—from any other.

The only way to *see* Truth is by noticing if your mind is leaning.

If your mind leans, it's because you see something "out there," apart from yourself. It's becoming lost in thought and imagination. It's being removed from immediate experience.

Notice what your mind is actually doing now. You don't have to seek to do this. You're already fully equipped. You don't have to go anywhere or do anything special. Simply make *just seeing* your intention. That's all.

To awaken is not to hold the idea of awakening. You can't practice waking up. And you can't fake it or imitate it. You have to actually want to wake up.

You're the one you can count on. You're not other-dependent. Everything you need is here now. Just rely on *thus*—immediate, direct experience.

You're the final authority. Whether you awaken or not is completely up to you.

Appendix
Dependent Arising

The Buddha's teaching on how ignorance and intention are linked to duhkha via a twelve-link chain is called Dependent Arising (*pratityasamutpada*). He said,

Dependent upon ignorance arise dispositions; dependent upon dispositions arises consciousness; dependent upon consciousness arise mind and body; dependent upon mind and body arise the six senses; dependent upon the six senses arises contact; dependent upon contact arises feeling; dependent upon feeling arises craving; dependent upon craving arises grasping; dependent upon grasping arises being; dependent upon being arises birth; dependent upon birth arise old age and death, grief, lamentation, suffering, dejection, and despair. Thus arises the entire mass of suffering.

However, from the utter fading away and ceasing of ignorance, there is ceasing of dispositions; from the ceasing of dispositions, there is ceasing of consciousness; from the ceasing of consciousness, there is ceasing of mind and body; from the ceasing of mind and body, there is ceasing of the six senses; from the ceasing of the six senses, there is ceasing of contact; from the ceasing of contact, there is ceasing of feeling; from the ceasing of feeling, there is ceasing of craving; from the ceasing of craving, there is ceasing of grasping; from the ceasing of grasping, there is ceasing of being; from the ceasing of being, there is ceasing of birth; from the ceasing of birth, there is ceasing of old age and death, grief, lamentation, suffering, dejection, and despair. And thus there is the ceasing of this entire mass of suffering.

The Buddha described this chain in terms of bondage and liberation. Bondage is the taking hold of any link of this chain (and thus the entire chain); liberation is the letting go of the chain. This letting go comes through *seeing*.

In this teaching, the Buddha points out what our actual experience is—that all things arise together, or dependently. Nothing appears by itself; everything we experience appears in a context and against a backdrop of other things that are dependent on and conditioned by each other.

A literal translation of the Buddha's words would be, "When this arises, that becomes." In other words, the Buddha never spoke of things as they are, since this is the very delusion we suffer from in the first place. He spoke of things as they have come to be in *this moment*, dependent on other things. When the sun rises, we have daylight. The Buddha would further remind us that these two things are always found together. Sunrise and daylight are not exactly two, but inextricably linked together.

In everyday life, however, the idea that all things come intimately joined is not at all obvious to us. This ignorance is what keeps us in bondage.

The twelve-link chain the Buddha spoke of is not a progression through time or space, as if link one leads to link two, and so on. Rather, if you pick up any one of these links, you have the whole chain—not in a temporal sequence, but all at once.

In the chart on page 175 the chain is presented as a straight line going from link one to link twelve. I've presented it this way for the sake of easy reading and comprehension. But a truly accurate picture would array the twelve links in a circle, like the numbers on the face of a clock.

Let's look at this chain in detail. We'll start with ignorance, which is considered the first link. Ignorance is like a black hole that sucks everything into it, even illumination. Thus we can't see it, at least not directly.

One of the characteristics of ignorance, then, is that we're ignorant of our ignorance. This puts a pernicious spin on our predicament.

There are two kinds of ignorance: blindness and self-deception. Blindness is ignorance of the basic realities of existence: impermanence, duhkha, and selflessness. (Buddha called these the "three marks of existence.") Self-deception is our belief that we can know intellectually what things are. "Oh! That's water," we say. "Hydrogen and oxygen." And then we dismiss the actual experience of this moment. (But if you really want to *know* what water is, just take a drink, or go for a walk in the rain, or take a swim.)

In short, we're simply confused about this moment. As Huang Po said, in our ignorance we reject actual experience in favor of what we think. Thus we posit a self in our thought, and we see permanence where there isn't any.

If instead we would attend to this moment, we would *see* that nothing actually arises, persists, or dies as a separate entity. This is what we truly can *know*—but we ignore it and suffer greatly as a result.

This moment is complete unto itself. There's nothing lacking in this moment. If we would actually *see* this moment for what it is, we would *see* all of space and time as nothing other than here and now.

In ignoring *this*—our actual experience—the mind no longer rests quietly in Wholeness, but begins to lean. The Buddha called this "disposition of mind," or intention. This forms the second link on the chain. Any actions that come out of such a mind are willed.*

We routinely act out of intent, out of a leaning mind. Nature, acting out of the Whole, does not. We commonly see things "out there" and go after them. Our mind is thus characterized by division and separation.

But the Whole functions differently. There's nothing "out there" for Mind to lean toward or away from. Thus the actions produced

---

* To understand the nature of willed action and how it binds us to duhkha, we must first look at the nature of action, or motion, in general. If I throw a ball, it will continue to move at the same speed and in the same direction I threw it, without stopping or changing course, unless it's acted upon by some other force. This would be obvious if we were in outer space. On earth, of course, the ball would just fall to the ground and roll to a stop. This is because the ball is being acted upon by the force of gravity. This is just simple physics.

When we see the ball bounce and roll to a stop, however, we tend to think the action is over. But only the ball has stopped. The action we took doesn't stop at all. When the ball hit the ground it jostled the soil and the grass and it converted its energy of motion to heat. Even though the ball comes to rest, the energy that once moved it is still here; it's been converted into heat and dispersed. It will continue to disperse, but it won't disappear.

My point is that the energy, or action, doesn't stop at all. Ever. Through innumerable transformations, it just continues on and on and on. This is how things are. Nothing stops. This is the nature of Reality. Indeed, this is the nature of Mind—pure, unending movement.

But here's where it gets critical. We might think that by tossing a ball we initiate an action, but this is merely an arbitrary point in a beginningless line of action. It's important to understand that a line of action, or movement, or energy that momentarily manifests as, for example a ball being thrown, has no discernible beginning. What *is* discernible is when intention steps into a line of action. To the awakened, this qualitatively changes the picture, and the change is total. It's the difference between freedom and bondage as defined by the Buddha. Simply put, willed action is radically different than unwilled, or natural action.

170

by Mind—the Whole, or nature—are radically different in essence (though not always in appearance) from acts of human will.

Nature acts out of the Whole, without any effort or intent. Through innumerable transformations, the Whole continues as beginningless and endless action and reaction. Intention steps into the natural flow of action and attempts to control it. This is the source of duhkha.

When in ignorance a mind imagines "that, out there," it leans toward it or away from it. This disposition of mind involves discrimination, the next link of the chain. This third link is also known as consciousness.

Consciousness divides Reality. It conceptualizes it, packages it, and explains it to itself. Then in our ignorance, we think it's taking readings on things "out there."

In Buddhism, consciousness is sometimes depicted as a monkey in a tree full of flowers. "Oh! I'll take that one, and that one, and that one." With consciousness, there's this, that, and the next thing. The world is continuously being divided up in various ways.

In our everyday view, we think that the world is out there, separate and persistent, and we think of consciousness as a sort of unifying action, a linking of pieces or parts. From such a view, your consciousness is taking in this book—visually, tactilely, and even audibly as you turn the pages.

To awakened people, however, the picture is reversed. What is actually experienced is always a seamless Whole. Consciousness divides it. And, of course, the most basic division is "me" and "everything else," self and other.

Consciousness not only divides the world spatially, it also divides it temporally. We thus imagine past, present, and future, and the persistence of separate objects.

Conscious experience is very much like a movie. It's just one moment—one still—after another. But because these seem to occur in rapid succession, we adopt the contradictory belief that there are particular, persistent things out there that nevertheless change. For this reason, the Buddha called this link "rebirth consciousness," a sense that objects persist, being reborn moment after moment.

Link four, mind and body, and link five, the senses, comprise the delusion that *we ourselves* are particular, persisting things. Each of us conceives of a particular body, then imagines that this body supports a particular consciousness. Along with these come the senses and the organs associated with them. According to Buddhist teachings, there are six senses: the five we are already familiar with and the mind. Each sense is paired with a sense organ: eyes with sight, ears with hearing, nose with smell, tongue with taste, body with touch, and mind with thought.

Once we conceive of objects as "out there," a persistent body and mind as "in here," and a set of sense organs to bridge the gap between the two, we have the illusion of contact or connection. This is link six. From our common, deluded standpoint, we think we're connected to a world "out there."

The great Zen master Pai-chang said, "If you realize there is no connection between your senses and the external world, you will be enlightened on the spot." There can be no connection because there are no separate things to be connected.

It's possible to experience directly what Pai-chang describes here. To *see* in this way is utterly liberating.

In our delusion—our sense of connection with things out there—we react emotionally. This is the seventh link, feeling.

Dependent upon feeling arises links eight and nine, craving and desire. This is the need to grab certain objects "out there" and bring them closer, and to keep others at a distance or push them away. With desire comes grasping, the ninth link of the chain. We want to hold onto what we love, and to grab hold of what we dislike and hurl it away from us. This link has also been called "the hardening of craving," or "attachment."

There are two forms of grasping. First there is the grasping at sense objects. You see the object of your desire out there and you take hold of it.

The second kind of grasping is holding tight to belief. The Buddha identified three common types of belief. The first is belief in something "out there" that will set everything right and make everything perfect—a heaven or paradise. But even the nihilistic view that "after I die, that's it" is still a form of grasping onto such a belief. Grasping at any thoughts or opinions fits this category, since this grasping is an attempt to make sense of our existence.

A second kind of belief is belief that ritual or ceremony can somehow save us from pain, confusion, and ignorance. It's only in learning to *see* this very moment, as it has come to be, that liberation occurs—not in wearing robes or performing ritual acts.

The third belief we grasp at is the belief in a self, a permanent existence. This is the belief that's most deeply rooted in us, and that causes us the most pain.

And now we have the tenth link, being: persistence or existence. This in turn will link to ignorance, since, in Reality, nothing persists. But with being comes birth, the eleventh link, and with birth comes death, the twelfth link. Thus birth and death, the great problem we all face, are linked to the grasping of a self. This is duhkha in its most gripping and pervasive form.

But duhkha need not grip us. To *see* this moment as it comes to be—to *see* that all is fluidity, that nothing separate is born, and that nothing dies—is to break the chain of bondage.

Two Ways to View the Twelvefold Chain

Bondage is	#	Liberation is
to ignore the Reality of this moment. It is blindness to the direct perception that this moment neither arises, persists, nor perishes.	1 ignorance	to *see* the Reality of this moment. It is to perceive directly that this moment neither arises, persists, nor perishes.
instability of mind, caused by ignorance, that sets the mind to leaning. All actions produced by such a mind are willed.	2 intention	to *see* no substance in any object of mind. Hence the mind leans neither toward nor away. All actions produced by such a mind are unwilled.
to discriminate between separate objects of mind, and to see them as persisting from moment to moment.	3 conscious-ness	to *see* all mind objects as momentary and conditional.
to see a distinct, persistent, self-identical mind and body supporting consciousness. Thus a subject is discerned, along with its objects.	4 mind & body	to *see* no persistent mind or body— no subject—since there are no distinct and persistent mind objects available to perception.
to conceive a world of mind objects, external to the body and mind, as being taken in through the windows of the senses.	5 six senses	to *see* sensation as a function of Mind alone—that the objects of Mind are never external to Mind, but are always Mind itself.
to conceive that through sensation the subject makes contact with an objective world, "out there."	6 contact	to realize there's no connection or distinction between the senses and a world external to Mind.
to react emotionally to the objects of mind, while remaining isolated from them.	7 feeling	not being swept away by emotion. Since nothing is perceived as external to Mind, feeling is ever intimate.
to experience wanting and craving, since mind objects are conceived as being apart from "me," the subject.	8 craving	not to want. Since nothing is perceived as being "out there," there's no sense that anything is lacking.
to grasp at what appears "out there." It's the hopeless wish that this moment will either vanish or last.	9 grasping	to *see* all of experience as utter fluidity and, therefore, as nothing to grasp, own, or fear.
to conceive (believe in) the persistence (existence) of self and other.	10 being	to *see* all as stream.
to conceive (believe) that all beings have come into existence.	11 birth	to *see* that nothing is born.
to conceive (believe) that all beings will die.	12 death & duhkha	to *see* that nothing dies.

About the Author

Steve Hagen is a Zen priest, a long-time teacher of Buddhism, and the author of *How the World Can Be the Way It Is: An Inquiry for the New Millennium into Science, Philosophy, and Perception.*

Hagen began studying Buddhism in 1967, and in 1975 became a student of Zen master Dainin Katagiri, author of *Returning to Silence: Zen Practice in Daily Life.* He was ordained a Zen priest in 1979. Hagen later studied with a number of other teachers in Asia and Europe. In 1989 he received Dharma Transmission (endorsement to teach) from Katagiri Roshi.

Hagen lives in Minneapolis, where he lectures, teaches meditation, and leads retreats at Dharma Field Meditation and Learning Center. He is currently working on several books, and has edited a collection of Dharma talks by Katagiri Roshi.

You may write to Steve Hagen at
c/o Dharma Field
3118 West 49th Street
Minneapolis, MN 55410

The Tuttle Story: "Books to Span the East and West"

Most people are surprised when they learn that the world's largest publisher of books on Asia had its humble beginnings in the tiny American state of Vermont. The company's founder, Charles Tuttle, came from a New England family steeped in publishing, and his first love was books—especially old and rare editions.

Tuttle's father was a noted antiquarian dealer in Rutland, Vermont. Young Charles honed his knowledge of the trade working in the family bookstore, and later in the rare books section of Columbia University Library. His passion for beautiful books—old and new—never wavered throughout his long career as a bookseller and publisher.

After graduating from Harvard, Tuttle enlisted in the military and in 1945 was sent to Tokyo to work on General Douglas MacArthur's staff. He was tasked with helping to revive the Japanese publishing industry, which had been utterly devastated by the war. After his tour of duty was completed, he left the military, married a talented and beautiful singer, Reiko Chiba, and in 1948 began several successful business ventures.

To his astonishment, Tuttle discovered that postwar Tokyo was actually a book-lover's paradise. He befriended dealers in the Kanda district and began supplying rare Japanese editions to American libraries. He also imported American books to sell to the thousands of GIs stationed in Japan. By 1949, Tuttle's business was thriving, and he opened Tokyo's very first English-language bookstore in the Takashimaya Department Store in Ginza, to great success. Two years later, he began publishing books to fulfill the growing interest of foreigners in all things Asian.

Though a westerner, Tuttle was hugely instrumental in bringing a knowledge of Japan and Asia to a world hungry for information about the East. By the time of his death in 1993, he had published over 6,000 books on Asian culture, history and art—a legacy honored by Emperor Hirohito in 1983 with the "Order of the Sacred Treasure," the highest honor Japan bestows upon a non-Japanese.

The Tuttle company today maintains an active backlist of some 1,500 titles, many of which have been continuously in print since the 1950s and 1960s—a great testament to Charles Tuttle's skill as a publisher. More than 60 years after its founding, Tuttle Publishing is more active today than at any time in its history, still inspired by Charles Tuttle's core mission—to publish fine books to span the East and West and provide a greater understanding of each.